Praise for Previous Editions

"**Great. Maxine answers every conceivable question and then some....
I strongly recommend this book to all my students.**" —*Richard Wilde, Chair,
BFA Advertising and Graphic Design Department, SVA; Founding Partner, Wilde Design*

"**Read this book before you go to ad school. Max Paetro's advice
is timeless.**" —*Betsy Yamazaki, Executive Vice President, Creative Recruiter,
Marcus St. Jean*

"**When I started out wanting to be a copywriter, *How to Put Your Book
Together* was my 'Bible.' I remember lying on my parents' couch reading
this book, wondering how I was going to get the attention of that
elusive creative recruiter. Now that I am one myself, I know what all my
candidates are going through. So it's great to know that the 'How-to Bible'
is still here to guide them, just as it did me.**" —*Michele Daly, Global Creative
Talent Director, Y&R Brands*

"**Maxine Paetro makes a long overdue contribution to the agency world....
Hers is no stuffy, professorial tome. Instead, it's a conversationally written,
witty primer on the agency hiring ABCs.**" —*New York Daily News*

"**There are two ways to embark on a career in advertising: One, buy Maxine
Paetro's book. Two, buy a helmet. Number one is cheaper, faster, and
smarter.**" —*Ed McCabe, Hall of Fame Copywriter*

"**Max is terrific! This book is an invaluable tool for young people starting in
the creative side of business—full of important tips that could make the
difference in their approach to job interviews.**" —*Judy Wald, The Judy Wald Agency*

1

"Paetro's book is timeless...one of the classics of advertising brain building that reminds us there are no real rules, a few valuable guidelines, and lots of great common sense to take to heart if you want to make it as a creative." —*Deborah Morrison, Professor of Advertising, University of Oregon School of Journalism and Communication*

"The unfortunate pilgrim, drifting in the big city, can heed her guidelines in all aspects of job hunting....This book offers a positive and supportive attitude to those struggling with the bewildering prospect of the hunt." —*Advertising Techniques*

"This is a remarkable book. It speaks directly to the young person for whom the message is intended." —*Ron Seichrist, Founder, Portfolio Center and Miami Ad School*

"This book reads like a long, interesting chalk talk from one of advertising's great coaches. Maxine really knows what it takes to get a creative director's attention." —*Andrew Jaffe, AdWeek/The Clio Awards*

"It's a fabulous book. A great resource for someone who's trying to get into the business or someone who's already in the business and trying to do better work." —*Sandy Wade, The Sandy Wade Company*

"It took me several years to find a job as a copywriter. If this book were around in those days, I'm egotistical enough to believe it would have taken only seven days." —*Jerry Della Femina, CEO, Creative Director, Della Femina, Rothschild, Jeary and Partners*

HOW TO PUT YOUR BOOK TOGETHER AND GET A JOB IN ADVERTISING

NEWLY REVISED EDITION

Also by Maxine Paetro

Manshare

Babydreams

Windfall

*The Magnificent Shattered Lives of Bobby Darin
and Sandra Dee* (with Dodd Darin)

With James Patterson

The 4th of July

The 5th Horseman

The 6th Target

7th Heaven

The 8th Confession

The 9th Judgment

Swimsuit

Private

HOW TO PUT YOUR BOOK TOGETHER AND GET A JOB IN ADVERTISING

NEWLY REVISED EDITION

Maxine Paetro

Illustrations by Giff Crosby

W. W. Norton & Company

New York • London

For information about permission to reproduce selections from this book,
write to Permissions, W. W. Norton & Company, Inc., 500 Fifth Avenue, New York, NY 10110

For information about special discounts for bulk purchases, please contact W. W. Norton Special Sales
at specialsales@wwnorton.com or 800-233-4830.

Composition and book design by Matt Bouloutian & Vivian Ghazarian, Modern Good
Manufacturing by Courier Westford
Production Manager: Leeann Graham
Electronic Production: Joe Lops

Library of Congress Cataloging-in-Publication Data

Paetro, Maxine.
How to put your book together and get a job in advertising / Maxine Paetro. —Newly rev. ed.
    p. cm.
 Includes bibliographical references and index.
 ISBN 978-0-393-73285-6 (pbk.)
1. Advertising—Vocational guidance. I. Title.

HF5828.4.P33 2010
659.1023—dc22
                                    2010005049
ISBN 13: 978-0-393-73285-6 (pbk.)

W. W. Norton & Company, Inc., 500 Fifth Avenue, New York, N.Y. 10110
www.wwnorton.com
W. W. Norton & Company Ltd., Castle House, 75/76 Wells St., London W1T 3QT
1 2 3 4 5 6 7 8 9 0

To those of you who are working on your books.

And to all my friends and associates who taught me what I know about advertising.

CONTENTS

ACKNOWLEDGMENTS

My special thanks to my fabulous editor, Andrea Costella, and my multitalented researcher and coordinator, Lucy López. Without them, this newly revised edition would still be spinning on my hard drive.

My enduring thanks to these wonderful people who helped me put the original version of this book together: My friends and co-workers at Foote, Cone & Belding, Ogilvy & Mather, Young & Rubicam, and Dancer, Fitzgerald, Sample, especially Billy Foster, who designed the first cover, Marshall Karp, who provided a sounding board, and all of the beginning copywriters and art directors who let me use examples from their books. Also the late Ed Buxton, who blessed, edited, published, and sold the original edition.

For their help in successive editions from 1980 to 2002, I want to thank my friends at Saatchi and Saatchi Worldwide, the "kids" who came through our creative training programs, and all of the students and job-seekers who contributed their stories, résumés, advice, and promotional ideas. Thanks too to Bruce Bendinger and Lorelei Davis of the Copy Workshop, who published ten editions of this book, Giff Crosby for his humorous and accessible illustrations, and Flinn Dallis of Leo Burnett, who has supported this book from the very beginning. I also want to thank my friends and former colleagues who have kept me in the talent recruitment loop: Marie Arteca, Ginny Howsam, Pippa Seichrist, Nancy Temkin, Carol Vick, and Betsy Yamazaki; and fellow headhunters Michele Daly, Leslie Kay, Dany Lennon, Kathy Primozic, Cathy St. Jean, Sandy Wade, and Jill Weingarten.

And special thanks to my very good friend James Patterson, who showed me his junior book when he was looking for his first job in advertising, and many years later gave me space at JWT when he was Worldwide Creative Director and I was working on a book of my own.

The edition of this book you now hold in your hands has been advanced by valuable contributions of old and new friends: Marie Arteca, David Baldwin, Rick Boyko, Giff Crosby, Flinn Dallis, Michele Daly, Heidi Ehlers, Bertrand Garbassi, Charles Hall, Jim Hord, Ginny Howsam, Marshall Karp, Leslie Kay, Dany Lennon, Ed McCabe, Dan Mountain, James Patterson, Steve Penchina, Kathy Primozic, Neil Raphan, Pippa Seichrist, Brian Shembeda, Lauren Staff, Cathy St. Jean, Nancy Temkin, Ben Thoma, Carol Vick, and Betsy Yamazaki.

And many thanks to Curtis Clarkson at *CMYK* and Yash Egami from *One: A Magazine*, who were kind enough to let us use essays that originally ran in their fine publications.

I'm very grateful to the very talented people who sat down in front of their blank screens and wrote dazzling, insightful, practical, and wise essays for this book: David Baldwin, Tom Cunniff, Greg DiNoto, Jim Durfee, Doreen Dvorin, Heidi Ehlers, Jeffrey Epstein, George Felton, Jack Foster, Cliff Freeman, Roz Goldfarb, Jeff Goodby, Dean Hacohen, Charles Hall, Jhames Holley, Wayne Johnson, Lee Kovel, Leora Mechanic, Deborah Morrison, Jim Mountjoy, James Patterson, Robin Raj, Amy Krouse Rosenthal, Helen Klein Ross, Ron Seichrist, Susan Spiegel Solovay, Helayne Spivak, Luke Sullivan, and Eric Weber.

Great thanks to the One Club in New York and to department heads, instructors, and placement people at the Portfolio Center, the University of Texas, Syracuse University, the School of Visual Arts, the Fashion Institute of Technology, the L.A. Art Center, The Creative Circus, and the Miami Ad School for inviting me to speak on their campuses and to the students of these schools who have taught me, taken what I've dished out, and written in with their questions.

We want to thank the instructors who gave our cover competition as a class assignment and the designers and art directors who competed from Academy of Art University, Adhouse, the Art Institute of Pittsburgh, Brainco, the College of Imaging Arts & Sciences at Rochester Institute of Technology, Kean University, Kendall College of Art and Design, Kennesaw State University, the Miami Ad School, Minneapolis College of Art and Design, Pratt, Savannah College of Art and Design, The Creative Circus, Universidad Anahuac México Sur, University of Alabama Birmingham, University of Muhamammadiyah Yogyakarta in India, University of Nebraska at Lincoln, University of Oregon, University of Texas at Austin, University of West Florida, Valencia Community College, and Virginia Commonwealth University.

Our congratulations and appreciation to our first-place winner, Alan Rayner of Valencia Community College, whose winning entry is the cover of this book, and second and third place winners, David Levine and Quinn Lindgren of Miami Ad School in San Francisco, for their excellent submissions.

I cannot thank Giff Crosby, my friend of more than thirty years, creative director, and cartoonist extraordinaire, enough. My thanks to him for updating and creating another round of apt and funny illustrations for the newly-minted edition of this book.

PREFACE

In 1978, I was the creative department recruiter at Foote, Cone & Belding, New York. The agency wasn't exactly like Sterling Cooper of *Mad Men*, but remnants of the sixties remained. Women worked on cosmetics and other "female" products. We had cigarette accounts and did TV commercials for them. I had a film projector in my office—and personal computers had not yet been invented. This is true!

There were very few schools teaching portfolio classes back then, and most of the "kids" who were looking for creative jobs had little idea about what the contents of a "book" should be.

So, based on talks I had given and a whole lot of questions from students, I wrote *How to Put Your Book Together and Get a Job in Advertising*. I wanted to help would-be writers and art directors cut down the time it took to prepare themselves and their books and to find the right job.

Today there are many terrific schools that specialize in teaching advertising to creative people, and computers have replaced magic markers, press-type, and other artifacts of the early days. Most everyone who dreams of getting a creative job in advertising today knows that they must have a "book" of speculative ads with headlines, visuals, and tag lines. But portfolios have changed in ways we couldn't have imagined even ten years ago.

When I last revised this book in 2002, the portfolio format of choice was "the mini-book," an 8" x 10" or even smaller collection of well-crafted and edited spec ads that were relatively cheap to have copied and bound at Kinko's, to be mailed or handed out at portfolio reviews or job interviews. We were questioning the use of CDs for this purpose, because recruiters still brought books physically to creative directors to review and most of those creative directors still wanted to hold ads in their hands.

Mini-books haven't completely vanished. Physical "interview books" are still requested at portfolio reviews and often when you land a one-on-one conversation with a creative director— but for reach and convenience, the tangible "book" has been utterly usurped by the pdf and the URL.

Recently I sent out a questionnaire to creative directors at big and small agencies across the country. When asked what form the portfolio should be in now, 100% of them wanted creative kids to have a Web site of their work so that they could review "books" in their office without having to trip over portfolio cases on their way to their desks. These creative directors say they like to bookmark Web sites they want to return to, and they forward URLs to their associates, even print out a pdf if they want a hard copy of an ad under review.

Just as the cover of this book shows an icon of a portfolio case that you may never have, the words *book* and *portfolio* will be used interchangeably throughout the text to mean your compilation of speculative ads. And although spec ads have gone from hand-drawn and actual to computer-generated and virtual, and even though advertising has come a long way from billboards painted on the sides of barns, the point of advertising hasn't changed a whit. And that's why the principles that guided beginning creative people when I wrote this book more than thirty years ago are still valid today.

Advertising must sell the client's product, service, or image. Or as advertising people have been saying for decades, "It's not creative unless it sells."

In these times of economic shortfall and the briefest attention spans in world history, advertising dollars have to work harder and faster and better. The Internet, interactive advertising, social media, and other venues yet to be invented are part of your now and your future. It is your job to be aware of advancements in technology and new sensibilities.

Even though ads go out to millions, they must reach individuals logically and emotionally in order to sell them on the product you are advertising. Your book must also win over another consumer, the one who might give you a job because he or she believes that you can create advertising that is smart and persuasive and original.

The first assault on the ad business is not for the chicken-hearted.

You can expect obstacles, disappointment, and infuriating inconsistency on the part of your evaluators. *It's very hard to get a creative job in an advertising agency, even if you are talented and have a good book.*

I'm telling you this not only because it's true, but because creative job seekers and agency "gatekeepers" have urged me to divulge this fact right up front.

If what you read in this book discourages you from pursuing a career in advertising, I'm glad I've saved you from what might have been years of frustration. Don't feel bad about this, should it happen.

As we sometimes say, "Hey. It's only advertising." And we mean it.

The advertising business is just a business—a very small business, although a very visible one. That's why so many people want to be in it and why so few people get in. But for those who are suited to it, it's the very best business in the world.

MAXINE PAETRO
August 2010

HOW TO PUT YOUR BOOK TOGETHER AND GET A JOB IN ADVERTISING

NEWLY REVISED EDITION

INTRODUCTION

I have never written a word of advertising copy, nor have I designed an ad or come up with an advertising idea.

What I have done in the course of my twenty-plus years in advertising has been to manage the creative departments of several large advertising agencies and to place or hire or recommend to be hired a whole lot of copywriters and art directors. In the process I have seen many, many thousands of books.

I wish I could, but I can't actually teach you how to become a copywriter or an art director. (I assume you have decided on an advertising career and have taken courses in advertising.) My purpose with this book is to help you become aware of what makes a great ad, help you think through the advertising process, give you some guidelines on how to present your work in the best possible light, assist you in getting to and impressing people who've seen as many portfolios as I've seen, and help you land a job.

The original *How to Put Your Book Together* grew out of talks I'd given to students at art schools and universities as a recruiter. This newly revised edition picks up from those talks and continues with the latest questions asked by a new generation of future advertising people, with up-to-the-minute answers given by new names in the industry as well as veteran top-dogs.

As before, the questions are from beginning copywriters and art directors, or those wanting to break into the business. The answers are mine and those of creative people who agreed to be interviewed, wrote essays, answered questionnaires, and generally have made their knowledge available to you and me. Although media are changing at the speed of light, the basics of creating advertising, speculative ads, and the job-getting process haven't changed.

The information in this spanking-new revision concerns first-year issues. In Part I, I define concepts and campaigns for those who have just begun to ask what this portfolio thing is all about. And there are new questions and answers that I hope will help those about to graduate, those who are about to enter or have already entered the tougher-than-ever entry-level job competition. As you put your book together, you may find that what some think is a big idea, others find derivative or dumb. I will address this maddening conundrum, and at the same time help you nail down the basics before you overturn the rules of conventional wisdom.

Part II addresses all aspects of getting a job, from résumés, cover letters, and business cards to interview etiquette and follow-up.

As I've done since the first edition of this book, I've invited creative heads of some of the top agencies around, headhunters, creative managers, and junior creative people to write essays and supplement the text of this book with their comments, their stories, and examples from their portfolios. The contributions of these generous people are of enormous value, and I'm delighted to pass their wisdom on to you in Part III, "A Little Help from Some Friends."

Finally, it is important to understand that in a business as subjective as advertising, there are often no right or wrong answers. But I think you will agree you have to know the rules in order to break them.

I hope you will incorporate the advice you get from this book with what you believe is right for you and, in the process, form your own good judgment.

If you can do that, you will have a better chance of getting your first job in advertising.

PART I
HOW TO PUT YOUR BOOK TOGETHER...

YOUR BOOK: THE BASICS

Advertising agency creative directors and recruiters are looking for the very best thinkers they can find. Principally, what they want to see in your book are *advertising ideas that sell products*.

When you hear a person described as being "conceptual," this is what the speaker means. There is an expectation that both copywriters and art directors should be conceptual.

At some point, agencies look for different skills in copy and art, but for the moment, let's talk about this thing called *concept*.

A concept, very simply, is an *idea*.

In terms of advertising, it's the central theme that underlies your advertising. It's the premise that is the foundation of your ad and your campaign.

The best way to express your concept is in a *campaign* format.

A campaign is a series of ads for a product (or service or company) that work individually and cumulatively to communicate the advertiser's message to the consumer.

First, a simple example: "Got Milk?" This campaign, created by Goodby Silverstein & Partners, reminded people in a variety of creative ways that there are times when you really need to have milk.

The concept, the idea, remained the same in each ad. But the ads, part of the same set, changed visuals each time. That's a decent illustration of a campaign.

Interestingly enough, there's a second campaign for milk created by Bozell—the "milk mustache." This campaign worked "to establish milk as a contemporary beverage alternative." Again, there is a unifying visual, celebrities wearing their milk mustaches. Along the way, the client decided to combine them.

Two more clear examples of long-running campaigns are those for two credit card brands— VISA and MasterCard. Even though these two products are obviously very similar—identical, really—each developed a different and meaningful campaign approach.

VISA tells you they are "everywhere you want to be" in a variety of desirable ways. They connect with all the fun places you can spend money with a VISA card. Meanwhile, MasterCard talks about being part of your life with their "priceless" campaign—and the line "There are some things money can't buy. For everything else, there's MasterCard."

Before we leave these campaigns, think about that set of words that comes at the end of the commercial or is at the bottom of the print ad. "Got Milk?" And "It's Everywhere You Want to Be."

What's hard at work here is a device called a *tag line*, sometimes called a base, theme, or logo line. Used as a positioning statement, this line tells the consumer how the advertiser wants his product or company to be perceived, and this message is delivered in a neat package the consumer can take with him.

A tag line also serves as a signature for the advertiser, thereby helping you, the consumer, link up all the ads you've seen for this product or company so that the effect of each ad is enhanced by your memory of the whole campaign.

Not all campaigns use a tag line, but for your purposes, you may find it a useful technique for pulling your ads together into a campaign. Very often, if you have a good tag line your ads may almost create themselves.

Can you think of some concepts that are so big, the agency could create (or "pool out") additional advertising around that concept for years? Does the advertiser use a tag line?

How about "Have It Your Way," a long-running campaign for Burger King, "Red Bull Gives Your Wings" for Red Bull, "I'm Loving It" for McDonalds, "Moving Forward" for Toyota, "The Few, the Proud, the Marines," for the USMC, and the famed "Just Do It" for Nike, which now uses these taglines: "Leave Nothing" for Nike Football and "Believe in the Run" for Nike Athletic.

A concept, very simply, is an idea.

Analyze your favorite campaigns.

Look at tag lines and see which ones effectively sum up a campaign idea and give the consumer a phrase to remember.

Consider how tag lines can work for you.

And now . . . back to your book.

When we look at it, we want to see that you can come up with concepts and expand your ideas into campaigns.

Now, don't think that a technically complete campaign—three ads for the same product—is sufficient. You've all seen enough advertising to simply imitate a campaign by doing three similar ads in a series.

If you do that, the person who is reviewing your book is going to doze off. You need to come up with fresh ideas that jar that person awake. You want him to go tearing down the hall with your book under his arm shouting, "Let's give this kid a job!"

But putting together a book that gets people excited is hard to do.

How are you going to do it? Well, having talent is a must.

Being clever distinguishes you.

Being thorough is your starting point.

YOUR GOOD FRIEND, DRANO

To do good ads, you must be on very good terms with your products. You have to know what you're talking about and to whom you're directing your message.

That's why I suggest you *concentrate on products you know or products you want to know more about*, because the more you know about your product, the more you care about it, the more likely you are to have an inspired idea. And the truer your ads will ring.

To get started, pick a product you know.

Check out your medicine chest or the cabinet under your kitchen sink. Got any friends in there? Okay. Choose one. Say hello, and if you feel like it, give it a friendly pat.

Then think through what made you buy that product. When you know why you bought that product, you're on your way to coming up with an idea that will convince someone else to buy it.

Choose products you know.
Here's one source of inspiration.

Now ask yourself these questions:

- In what ways is your product similar to others in its category?
- In what ways is it different?
- What benefit does your product offer?
- What (truthful) promise can you make about your product that will differentiate it from others in its category?
- What is the "advertising problem" you're trying to solve?
- Who buys your product now? Should you be addressing the same consumer? Or should you focus on, expand, or change your target?

"Oh, no," you might be thinking. "I don't have to know that stuff. That's account exec territory."

Sorry, but knowing your product—what it has to offer, what competes with it, and who you can persuade to buy it—is absolutely fundamental to the process of doing advertising. You shouldn't even think of executing your ad until you've got some answers to these questions.

Here's another.

In an advertising agency, this foundation work is often called *positioning* the product and developing a *strategy* for the advertising.

In real life, the account executive on your account will be key to this part of the process and will work with you to help you arrive at these reference points.

No one expects you to have a degree in marketing, but since you must have some form of this basic information before you start to do your speculative ads, you'll have to pour the foundation yourself.

Now, how about doing some research on your product?

Advertising agencies talk to consumers. You can do the same.

The people who work in an agency's planning department probe the marketplace for insight into the consumer's tastes, values, loyalties, preferences. They design questions, analyze data, and interpret it for use by the creative department.

One frequently used research tool is the *focus group*. In an informal setting, volunteer consumers answer questions about a specific product or product category. Sometimes they look at "spec" advertising, answer questions about it, and as a result, the ads may be abandoned. Sometimes new ideas are born.

What am I suggesting now? That you become a planner? Don't worry. This is painless. Even fun.

Think about doing some research on your product.

You can certainly use the Internet, blogs, Web polls—and this is probably where you gen nexters will start, but old fashioned methods are your friend, so please don't abandon them.

Go to your neighborhood supermarket and ask the manager why one brand of dog food outsells the competing brands. Study the competition. Read the labels. Take notes. Discuss your chosen products with family members, roommates, unsuspecting strangers in the pet food section.

Make new friends. Get some conversations going. Someone's offhand remark could spark that illuminating idea.

I know getting this involved with the product seems like a lot of work. It is a lot of work. And no one is expecting you to have all the answers. What we're hoping is that starting now you'll train yourselves to ask the questions.

Someday this process will be automatic. Upon meeting your new brand, your brain will strip-search it so fast, it won't even feel your fingerprints. Trust me on this. All good creative people—whether they get their marketing information in a formal or informal way, through a hundred-page strategic brief or a hundred well-chosen words with the client—think "product" and "consumer" before they think "headline" and "visual."

Get into a good habit now. Knowing the product and understanding your prospective consumer can help you come up with stronger ideas—ideas with impact. The better the ideas in your portfolio, the better the chance some creative director is going to say "Welcome to our agency."

Your ideas must have impact.

Q. What products should be represented in my portfolio? Should I work on a variety of accounts?

A. It would certainly simplify things if there were an official list of product categories that you should cover. Then you could check off this list as you go, and when the list was done, you would be, too.

But there is no such list.

People judging your book care about the quality of your ideas, and they care about your craftsmanship. Showing that you can work on a variety of products suggests to the person reviewing your book how your talents might be applied to the agency's client list.

And now, here's something new to think about.

While most people who look at your book won't have a product checklist in mind, they may go back over the whole of your book—even if it's very, very good—and consider the degree of difficulty you set for yourself in problem-solving.

In a competitive situation, your book will be ranked accordingly.

It's kind of the way diving and skating competitions are judged in the Olympics. Straight tens go to the athletes who do the tough maneuvers perfectly. Easy maneuvers, even if perfectly done, earn only eights.

As mentioned before, you're going to choose products you know or want to know. But I wouldn't suggest filling up your book exclusively with ads for cameras and motorcycles just because you love high-tech hard goods. A one-category book is drawing a pretty small box around yourself, don't you think? I'd suggest that you increase your range a bit. Is there a brand of detergent you can relate to? Are you dead loyal to Clean 'n' Shiny shampoo? Is there an antacid you always reach for when you've got a nasty stomach?

Maybe. But you don't want to do ads for an antacid, you say? All those shampoo ads look the same. You can't do good ads for detergents.

Tell that to Alka Seltzer, with the famed "plop plop fizz fizz." And tell it to Cheer. Bushels of awards have been won for the advertising for these two products, as well as for scouring pads, tomato sauce, and dog food.

Not long ago, Tide was a winner in the print category of award shows with their "Stains Don't Stand a Chance" campaign. Saatchi has also done wonders with Tide-To-Go, in a particularly entertaining spot where a gentleman in an interview is overshadowed by an obnoxiously loud-talking stain on his shirt. This also took home its share of awards.

But come to think of it, no award-winning shampoo advertising comes to mind. So here, I think, is an opportunity for you to distinguish yourself.

Here's what one advertising professional thinks about the question of what products you should choose to showcase in your book.

Dan Mountain, a poet and an award-winning former copywriter and creative director, offers the following tips on product category selection.

1. Pick a product you use every day, *a product you need but don't want*. Mouthwash, cereal, shoe polish. You choose.

2. Pick one product you buy quite often that you *want, don't need*. Candy bars, magazines, CDs, etc.

3. Pick a product that you don't buy more than once a year. It's a *considered purchase*. A car, a new phone, two weeks in the sun.

Ginny Howsam, a former executive headhunter, suggests a fourth type of product:

4. Pick a product you feel passionately about. Anything, so long as your feelings about it are strong.

THE WORLD'S TOUGHEST PRODUCT CATEGORY

That shampoo I mentioned, along with the antacid and the detergent, etc., fall into a category of products called packaged goods.

Packaged goods come in a box, tube, or a container of some sort—the package. You buy them in a grocery store or pharmacy.

Talking Stain says: Packaged goods ads
can win big at the awards shows.

Toothpaste, cleansers, baby peas—in fact all canned goods—are packaged goods.

You use the products up, and then you buy them again, like Band-Aids, for instance.

Now there's a packaged goods campaign that has truly stood the test of time. It was created by Young & Rubicam in 1976 and ran for over twenty years. As one of the most memorable and longest running campaigns in advertising, it was voted into the Clio Hall of Fame in 1991. And in 2007, after it was off air for ten years, Ogilvy decided to update the lyrics and bring back the classic Barry Manilow jingle everyone remembers: "I am stuck on Band-Aid Brand, 'cause Band-Aid's stuck on me."

Advertising for packaged goods represents several million dollars annually. Procter & Gamble alone spends billions of dollars a year in ads and commercials. About 75 percent of the ads you see are for packaged goods products, which means that doing advertising for clients that make packaged goods is big business for big agencies.

If I may take this thought a step further, the odds are pretty good that if you get into advertising, there's a packaged goods account somewhere in your future.

Now, to crank the difficulty factor up another notch, I'd like to introduce you to the word *parity*. While it's tough to make startling ads for a straight-up packaged goods product, it's even tougher to take on a parity product.

A parity product is one that is just about the same as all other products in its category—a "me-too" product.

Let's compare the two types of products.

For instance, Crest is a toothpaste. It's a packaged goods product. Crest toothpaste is also a parity product. It has virtually the same properties and ingredients as its other major competitors.

Crest White Strips, on the other hand, are a much more distinctive product with an obvious and immediate benefit.

It is easier for you to do an ad for Crest White Strips than it is for you to do an ad for Crest. The strips have a few product differences you can get your brain around.

With Crest, on the other hand, you really have to push to differentiate it from Colgate, or others in its category. And that gives you a chance to really show off your conceptual talent.

Your mission, should you choose to accept it, is to look at that toothpaste from all angles, uncover a unique but truthful selling idea, and then execute that idea in a dazzling way.

And that's tough to do.

Come up with a great campaign for Crest White Strips, and we're happy. Come up with a new idea for Crest toothpaste, and we're more than happy, we're a little stunned.

Creating advertising for parity products is a major challenge for people in the advertising business. They deal with products that have tiny or nonexistent differences, and yet they are expected to create advertising that gives the product a unique quality.

Sometimes the biggest difference between two products is the advertising. This is the stuff of which the cola and burger wars are made, and carving out a position for a parity product is very difficult.

But it can be done. That Cheer detergent campaign I mentioned was created by Leo Burnett and went something like this: A silent spokesman takes a lipstick-smeared hanky, puts it in a cocktail shaker of cold water and ice cubes, shakes it up for thirty seconds, and produces a clean hanky. "Nothing Washes Cleaner in Cold" is the line. This amusing and solid campaign successfully ran for many years.

Ogilvy & Mather also blew everyone's minds with their Dove Evolution viral video for Dove products, where an average woman sits in front of a camera in a studio, and in fast forward, we see a crew of people do her hair and make-up and take photos.

The screen then turns into Photoshop view, where they elongate her neck, widen her eyes, thin out her jaw, and post her on an advertising billboard. We then read, "No wonder our perception of beauty is distorted . . . Take part in the Dove Real Beauty Workshop for Girls. Visit campaignforrealbeauty.com"

Together, Dove and Ogilvy created a self-esteem movement and a new view of what beauty really is. Can your shampoo and deodorant ads spark that kind of emotion?

Services also have parity—like insurance companies, banks, and airlines. For example, American Airlines, Delta Airlines, and United have parity in that they're all offering the same service and the same basic approach. "No frills," lower-fare airlines, like Southwest, AirTran, and JetBlue, have a different type of selling message—one that differentiates them from "the big boys."

So if we look at your book and we see ads that say Southwest is cheaper, we hope your execution is great because the "product" difference makes coming up with a concept relatively easy.

A QUIZ

Which one isn't a packaged good? (Take your time.)

Which one isn't a parity product?

And, finally, which one isn't a parity service?

Q. **What if you're not ready to take on a parity product or service?**

A. If you've tried, but the results are dull, back off for now.

Your objective is to set yourself as difficult a challenge in product selection as you can cope with. But most of us would rather see a book of ads for Crest White Strips and Southwest Airlines executed brilliantly than an entire book of detergent ads done in a boring but competent way.

Q. **There isn't a packaged goods client within a thousand miles of the place I call home and where I want to work. Do I have to do ads for packaged goods?**

A. Heck no. Flinn Dallis, former senior vice president for creative operations at Leo Burnett, has this advice: "Make your book match your market."

By which she means: if there is very little packaged goods business in your city of choice, do ads for insurance companies, brokerage firms, real estate companies, retail businesses, restaurants, and automotive products, as well as the consumer goods you'd just plain like to take a crack at. When in Chicago, think food.

On the West Coast, there are more retailers and computer companies on agency client rosters than there are in New York. And you will want your campaigns to include outdoor advertising.

There isn't a packaged goods account within 1,000 miles.
Do you still need to do ads for them?

Actually, an outdoor ad is even welcome in Gotham, where we don't have too many billboards on display. A concept that has impact at fifty-five miles an hour is impressive anywhere.

Bruce Bendinger, Creative Associate at Tamada Brown & Associates and owner and creative director at The Copy Workshop/First Flight Books, adds, "Make your book match your skills." He means: If your strength is posters for a rock concert or sales promotion pieces for your uncle's store, do those. Then you might want to pitch your book and yourself toward event marketers, hip design shops, sales promotion agencies, or even in-house advertising groups at places like The Gap or Starbucks. Go with what you know or want to know.

Ad great Steve Penchina suggests, "Pick your camp." If you don't want to work at a packaged goods agency, don't do packaged goods ads. Concentrate your efforts and your energy in getting into one of those agencies that are constantly cited in the award annuals—be they in Portland, Minneapolis, Manhattan, or Tuscaloosa.

Marie Arteca, formerly a big agency recruiter and now management recruiter for O'Hare & Associates, says, "Don't do packaged goods for the sake of doing packaged goods no matter where you live." She continues, "A great book is great for JWT and it's great for TBWA\Chiat\ Day. We're all looking for original thinking, expressed brilliantly. But don't wimp out when you pick your products. Show us you've got some teeth."

I'd like to sum up here with another quote from Flinn Dallis: "Make your book look like the job you want."

I think that's excellent advice.

To sum up:

In real life, advertising agencies have many different accounts, and each of those accounts must be approached in a custom-tailored way.

So—do ads for a variety of accounts. Show some range.

Work on products you understand—big brands and small, hard goods and soft.

Try to do at least one campaign for a parity product or service. This is where you will find your toughest challenges.

Consider doing a campaign for a packaged goods product.

While you won't get points for doing a C+ bar soap ad, an A+ bar soap ad says you're special.

Finally, no agency will turn you away because you haven't done packaged goods or parity products, or because you haven't covered every product category. A book of splendid, original, captivating ads transcends any niggling concerns about product selection.

Q. What types of products or accounts should I avoid?

A. Again, there are no rules here, but here are some categories where "spec" ads may not be able to compete favorably with the real thing. My thoughts:

It's risky to do spec campaigns for products with advertising so outstanding that your chances of doing better work are quite slim.

In other words, your spec ads won't look so good by comparison.

One of those products is Absolut Vodka. The long-running iconic Absolut campaign, which recently changed to "In an Absolut World," was a collection of elegant ads in which a swimming pool, a golf green, or some other witty visual effect was depicted in the shape of the Absolut bottle.

Each ad projected an iconic image of the product, involved the consumer in solving the visual puzzle, and summoned up recollections of other ads in the campaign. This is about as good as a campaign can get—to the point where some people even collect them.

It would be hard to beat the Absolut campaign.

I wouldn't go after Nike, either. Their image has been so impressed upon consumer America, we need only see their familiar "swoosh" logo and we call up rafts of Nike ads and television commercials from our memory banks.

Similarly, I wouldn't take on Apple, because they have managed to turn this into i-culture and those are some big shoes to fill.

Good luck.

Perhaps you can think of campaigns for other products or services that have achieved first-class, indelible brand identities. If you are going to do a spec campaign for one of these classic accounts, make sure your campaign is a killer.

It's very difficult to create brilliant "image" campaigns without the use of great photography, music, production values.

A definition: *Image advertising* reflects the personality or look a client's target consumer relates to, or wants to emulate.

Rather than appealing to logic (as does the Cheer campaign), it persuades by inviting consumers to picture themselves in the ad. Beauty and fashion accounts frequently use image advertising to project their message, as do cigarette, liquor, and beer accounts. When you think of Calvin Klein's advertising, or Dolce Gabbana or Lexus, I'll bet a picture and a mood comes to mind, but not a snappy line to take away.

The image ad usually depends on an intangible, emotional feeling expressed by an unusual graphic concept and rich production values. Most (although not all) great image campaigns are rooted in film, and this is why you, at home at your desk or keyboard, might be at a disadvantage.

Mercedes-Benz once gave us a herd of galloping rhinos. Pepsi, using the best television production money can buy, conveyed their message with great music, Britney Spears, or fancy trick-camera work.

More recently, Coca-Cola has given us the wonderfully animated Happiness Factory that takes us into the fantasy world where Coke is created.

While iPod's faceless silhouettes have made it to our TV screens by transforming well-known performing artists like Mary J. Blige, Coldplay, U2, and Eminem into living versions of their always colorful ads.

BMW also did an amazing job with their viral BMW Films, short action-packed stories starring the car, directed by the well-known Guy Ritchie and including other celebrities like Clive Owen and Madonna. Now that's branded entertainment.

You've got less than a few million dollars to spend and are creating campaign awareness from scratch. Can you make a big production idea (as opposed to a big selling idea) come alive in your book? Can you do it without ripping off images that have already appeared in print for another product? It's a heck of a challenge.

Advertising portfolios coming out of schools that specialize in portfolio development have become very sophisticated.

These books can cost their creators a thousand bucks or more to produce. Scrap photos are imported into Macs, sized up and down, and altered. Exotic typefaces abound. When there is an original concept behind these showy productions, images with impact can leap from that portfolio into a reviewer's mind.

So I'm not saying don't try to create a compelling image campaign, because this could be an area where success is equal to a home run. But remember—conveying image in spec print is hard to do well, and if you only do a fair job, it may not be worth doing.

Don't do too many campaigns for local retailers.

If we don't understand the local lore and you assume we know it, we may miss the point of your campaign. If you must do ads for the campus pizza hangout, keep in mind that Joe's Pizza doesn't run double page spreads in *Sports Illustrated*. Do a small space ad campaign instead.

Don't do too much public service advertising.

A public service ad is one that pleads a cause, solicits money, recruits volunteers, or in other ways performs a not-for-profit information service. "Don't Wear Fur," "Don't Do Drugs," and "Use Condoms" all fit into the public service category.

If parity products are on the high end of the difficult challenge scale, public service ads are on the low end. They are relatively easy to do because emotion is already built into the "product"; you don't have to create it. It's fine to do one public service ad or campaign for your book, but if your best headline is "Adopt These Puppies or We Will Kill Them," your book needs more solid work.

As with all rules, there are exceptions.

Charles Hall, professor at VCU Brandcenter and founder and designer of Fat Daddy Loves You Bath Couture, came up with this magnificent public service campaign. Picture a series of ads depicting steamy black and white close-ups; a women's bosom in a black lace bra, a stretch of creamy thigh gripped with a garter belt fastener, an exposed navel above lacy underwear. In tiny red letters that draw the reader in very close to the page is this caption: "This is not an invitation to rape me."

This is a great, moving, simple campaign that might actually change human perceptions. Charles did a strong public service campaign for a cause he cares about, and his caring shows. (Read his essay in Part III of this book.)

One public service campaign that people always seem to remember is the anti-smoking "Truth" campaign that shows young people taking on the big tobacco companies using unconventional techniques, such as stacking body bags outside of Philip Morris offices to show how many people cigarettes kill in one year. Powerful stuff.

If you decide to do a public service ad, do one for a cause that's important to you. Exploiting shock for shock's sake, and hitching a ride on the thing we fear most right now, is not reason enough to do a public service ad.

Q. **What do you like to see most in a book?**
What do you like to see least?

A. I like to see ads that feel like they came from the heart of the creator; ones that talk to a human being on a human level, ones that evoke an emotional response. I think of this kind of ad as having "heart."

An ad with heart will warm the reader, or scare him, or snap him to attention, or make his jaw drop, or make him laugh, or make him wonder.

And an ad with heart doesn't lie.

It supports its emotional message with facts, sometimes referred to as a "reason why." Sometimes as "permission to believe."

When a person reads an ad, he reads by himself. He (or she) should feel you are speaking just to him, not to a million other people at the same time. Your ads will have much more impact if you picture this individual reader in your mind.

Here's an example:

If you were writing a perfume ad, you could say, "This perfume is sexy." But Judy wrote, "Put It Where You Want to Be Kissed." See what I mean? That headline makes you feel something. Where do you want to be kissed?

Colleen, a beginning art director, did an ad for a new product she invented—a deep-cleansing soap. Her visual was two photos, one of a young woman and one of a newborn baby. Her headline was, "Your Skin Hasn't Been Clean Since the Day You Were Born."

Wow! Really? How come? She pulled me right into that ad by speaking to me. Her visual was compelling, and her few lines of copy described this new kind of soap. It made me focus on the condition of my skin.

Here's another great ad by Aline, a junior art director. The visual: a young girl reading a book on a field of grass covered by a shadow of what seems to be a gigantic flower. The product: Miracle-Gro. Simple yet smart; you can't go wrong with that.

I like humor that works.

Chris's campaign for an exotic pet shop shows a close-up of an alligator. The headline: "Sure, he'll catch a frisbee—if you tie a poodle to it."

Grant and Mike came up with this ad for Priceline. The visual shows a Hostess cupcake with a bride and groom wedding topper. The tagline reads "Priceline. Cheap. Like You." And it's clarified by the body copy: "Finding an inexpensive honeymoon suite has never been easier. With Priceline.com save up to 40% on 7,000 hotels in 1,300 cities." Gets your attention, makes you laugh, and communicates a selling message.

I like smart, simple, grabby demos that make the product the star of the campaign.

Michael and Curtis did this clever ad for Turtle Wax.

Picture a beautiful landscape. Upon close inspection, you realize that the landscape is a reflection in the finish of the side of a car. The headline: "Scenery by Mother Nature. View by Turtle Wax." A perfect demonstration of the product.

I like ads that are founded on an original idea.

Andrea and Matt created a campaign for Rose's Lime Juice based on the personality of a sour character named Rose.

Rose is never pictured, but alongside a vivid, stylized visual of the bottle is snarky copy like this: "I hate beautiful weather. And beautiful thoughts. And beautiful teeth. I hate holding hands and all that crap. Happiness is coming back for a five-year reunion and finding all of you bald. I hope you are all miserable." (Rose's graduation speech.)

The tag line is "Rose's Lime Juice. There Ain't Nothin' More Sour." I love this campaign because Andrea and Matt "get" the product and engage the consumer. They brought an ordinary product to life with intelligence and wit to create an original product personality.

I like ads that are well crafted.

I like visualizations and words that are honed, impactful, and reflect your individual point of view.

Kim and Bobby came up with this ad for Dial soap. Visual: an outstretched, naked male arm. Hovering around the armpit is a small hummingbird. The Dial logo is in the bottom corner. This lovely, simple visual gets your attention, and sells the product.

Some general advice:

Art directors: Unless it really is the best way to go, you know to break away from the standard adlike layout; headline on top, visual in the middle, body copy on the bottom. But beware of going too far off the wall in the other direction.

Layouts that have too many elements are hard to read.

Bizarre type in numerous fonts, colors, directions, and sizes confuses the message and therefore the reader.

You must communicate in order to sell, and no one likes to work hard to get your message. And, to state the obvious, for art directors, design counts as much as concept.

Copywriters: Really write! Create pictures in our minds.

Both of you: Come up with a headline that grabs, and a tag line that sums up your concept—one that gives your reader that little package to take home.

Now. What I like to see least: I don't like to see a book filled with pun headlines.

It's possible a very good pun may work, but if creating them is your first instinct, your ads may be so slick they don't stick.

If they don't stick, they can't move the consumer, and they can't sell the product.

Here are some examples of pun headlines.

"Glove Me Tender." Insert name of glove line in ad. "Call in the Infant Tree." Insert plant nursery name in ad.

Do these headlines make you feel anything? Would they induce you to buy anything? Do you get the feeling some of these headlines were written even before the product was selected?

A rule. Never be clever at your product's expense.

Once in a while, we see a pun that showcases the product, that is, really makes the product the star of the ad. Here's what I mean.

Two juniors I know came up with this ad for Life Savers. Visual: a clean, white page filled with colorful, bigger-than-life Life Saver candies. Headline: "Hole Sale."

To pay off the line, there's a coupon below that invites the consumer to buy two, get one free. This pun is about and for the product. So, a pun can be fun, but a whole book of puns signals heartless advertising.

I dislike the casual use of celebrity spokespersons.

If your chosen celebrity is very well matched to your product, okay, but just grafting a famous person onto your product doesn't impress anyone.

We want to see ideas.

Unless you're Gatorade, David Beckham isn't an idea. In real life, LeBron James might not be interested in selling your product, and even if he is, does he promote your message or make you think you don't need a message?

Celebrity artists, ditto. Be careful when your campaign depends on cartoons by Booth, Larsen, Schultz, or Groening or photos by Annie Leibovitz.

True, advertising people use celebrities and high-priced photographers all the time, but at this stage we're more interested in seeing your ideas—selling ideas, that is—and shortcuts can short-circuit the process.

The heartless ad: a friend to no one.

Heartless ads make me nuts.

This, the biggest problem we see in portfolios from New York to California and every state in between, is the result of picking up your pencil or turning on your computer too soon.

The scenario can go like this. You had an idea for a visual and you've created a campaign around it.

Or you heard a headline in your head last night, and now you've picked a product to fit the headline and you're off and running.

Starting with an execution first is a sure way of creating heartless ads, sometimes called "adlike objects." All the components of an ad are there: the headline, the visual, the body copy, and the tag line. Some of these elements can be kind of smashing.

But the piece still doesn't move anybody, and because nobody is moved, the ad doesn't sell.

Here's an example of a heartless ad for Gatorade. Visual: A jogger, jogging, and a product shot in the corner of the page. Headline: "More Miles per Gallon." The tag line: "Gatorade. The High-Octane Drink."

Well, what do you think?

Kind of clever, right? But do you feel anything? Do you get any sense that this writer understands you, the athlete, or that he is bringing anything new to your understanding of the product?

Compare this ad with one from the long-running campaign for Nike athletic shoes. Their message spoke to the part of each of us that hates to exercise. Then, Nike's theme line—"Just Do It." Feel that? Even now that Nike has branched off from the classic line, the new "Believe in the Run" is sure to follow in the footsteps of greatness.

Again. The ad-making process always begins with the product and consumer. The execution follows. While you might be able to get away with a few clever-but-heartless ads, a whole book of them is going to work against you.

What else do I like least?

Walking Strategy Statements

A "walking strategy statement"—another adlike object—is an ad with no craft. Like its cousin, the heartless ad, the walking strategy statement has a headline, a visual, and body copy, but it reads like a research report.

It has no zing. It strikes no chord.

I think this kind of work shows up when you've taken the opposite approach to doing your ads too fast.

In this case, you've paid so much homage to your strategy (the way the product should be marketed) that your "key fact" is right there in the headline—bald, naked, and wearing its hiking boots.

Here's an example. The ad is for Elan Frozen Yogurt. The visual is a product shot in the center of the page. The headline: "Tastes Great Like Häagen-Dazs. Takes Out Fat and Calories That Häagen-Dazsn't." The tag line seems to be yet another piece of the strategy: "Elan Frozen Yogurt. For Sundaes and Every Day."

Understand the strategy? Catch the pun? Feel anything?

If your book is filled with walking strategy statements, you've forgotten the consumer wants to feel a connection to the product. He isn't looking for a lecture.

Vulgar Advertising

Keep it clean. Sexist, racist, and crude ads offend more people than they persuade. I can't think of any ads that offend people into buying the products, can you?

I interviewed a writer once who had created, perhaps innocently, this ad for Lender's Bagels. "So Nice and Jewy" was her headline. I think there was actually a visual of bagels, like quoits, on someone's nose. (I'm not sure, because I think I blacked out for a moment.) This is a true story.

In short, bad taste is bad news. What else?

Sloppy Presentations

You don't care about your book and it shows.

Your Web site or interview book has a last-minute feel. Misspellings abound. Links don't work. Ads that should have been pruned or trashed still live. If you don't care enough to give your very best, please don't waste our time.

And what else?

Class Assignments

If you put class assignments in your book, they'd better be terrific—not filler where you didn't even get top grades. You'll be competing with other people from your class, so an interviewer may have seen similar better campaigns for the same product. Are you cocky? Lazy? Or what?

There's a competition going on here, remember?

Naturally, you have a lot of class assignments in your book. If you were awarded gold stars and stickers, by all means keep those ads in. As for the rest, please take my advice.

Close your book on your class assignments and come up with a killer ad on your own. Then use it to replace your half-good, class-assigned campaign for a local beer joint that is adding nothing but fluff to your book.

Get sharp or get left behind.

Bottom line:

I do like ads that have an original idea, that are executed with thought and craft, that strike a chord with the reader.

I don't like ads that are offensive, slick, or sloppy, or where you've solved your advertising problem by taking the easiest path.

Q. **What's a killer ad?**

A. A killer ad is simple, dramatic, memorable.

It has heart, a brain, and sometimes a funnybone.

A killer ad is based on an original idea. It stands the test of time.

When you see a killer ad, you wish you'd done it.

One particularly timeless ad that comes to my mind is the classic 1987 ad for Maxell recording tape. I'm sure you've seen the one. A man is sitting in a chair in front of his tape deck. The sound, like wind, is blowing back his hair, his tie, the lampshade. Every time I see this ad, I get enthralled anew. It's visual, conceptual, unforgettable, and it sells.

These days, "a killer ad isn't just an ad, it's a killer concept that extends across multiple platforms," says Helen Klein Ross, the writer of the blog AdBroad and a veteran writer/creative director at some of New York's and San Francisco's top ad agencies. A killer concept is designed to engage consumers wherever they are on the media landscape. A killer concept is one that really works on all the platforms where target consumers are. "Because," Ross says, "consumers are media-agnostic. They don't segregate media the way agencies do. They don't say 'Now I am reading a traditional print newspaper, but what's that sound? A text beep?

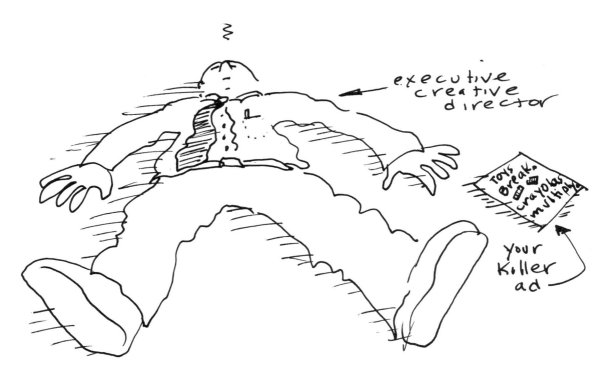

You want ads that kill. In a good way.

Let me switch promptly to mobile media!' They just live their lives, shifting from print to mobile to TV to digital without thinking. So to be successful brands must speak con vincingly and consistently throughout a complicated media universe."

A good example of a killer concept is Burger King's Whopper Sacrifice Campaign. Crispin Porter & Bogusky created a Facebook page that offers visitors a free Whopper when they "sacrifice" or defriend ten people from their friends list, using the catchy tag line "Friendship is strong, but the Whopper is stronger." Traffic to the Facebook page was built in part by ads in traditional media—a great example of how new advertising and old advertising work best together.

Would the Maxell campaign be a killer today? You bet. Why? Because it's a concept that can be extrapolated across platforms—on banner advertising, on YouTube, etc., and the idea affords creative opportunities in social media.

Then there are also killer integrated, "360" campaigns like the one developed by BBH/New York and @radical.media for Dry Axe antiperspirant. In addition to the more traditional print ads, commercials, and Web content, they created an entire MTV reality dating show called *GameKillers*, chronicling the mischief caused by a host of characters who are out to destroy a guy's chance of getting with his girl, all while he tries to remain cool. It's an advertisement that transformed into a television show, with "showmercials" interspersed throughout that actually sell the product. The idea behind these "360" campaigns is to creatively stretch the theme of the advertising campaign to take advantage of other marketing platforms and opportunities.

The world is chock full of great ambient ads. Take BBDO and Big Spaceship's "HBO Voyeur" campaign, for example. Eight individual stories involving murder, violence, romance, marriage, and cheating were created in fictional apartments and projected on the entire side of a building, where it appeared to spectators as if they were peering into the actual apartments where these stories were unfolding before them. Their tagline said it all: "See what people do when they think no one is watching." These stories, along with many others, could also be followed online.

And let's not forget killer ideas, like R/GA's Nike+ that teamed up with iPod to create the ultimate running experience: the iPod is synched to the shoe to track the runner's miles. And the social networking site created just for Nike+ owners that allows them to challenge and compete with other runners from all over the globe.

Need any more proof that advertising can change the world?

One former student I know tapes this killer spec ad right by his computer and uses it as a touchstone. Visual: a broken crayon. Headline: "Toys Break. Crayons Multiply."

This ad was created by creative director Gary Goldsmith (read his essay in Part III) when he, like you, was putting his book together.

Where to find more killer ads? Get your hands on some award annuals. The *One Show* book is one of the best. *Lürzer's Archive* takes you on an international advertising trip.

Or get the *Art Directors Annual*, the *Clio* book, or the *Communication Arts Advertising Annual*. Ad Age's *Creativity*, an e-zine, produces ten issues annually of current creative news, and *Adweek* showcases new work weekly. And get *CMYK*, an online and actual magazine featuring the best student work.

Here's how to rate your ads for killerhood:

- **Is your ad (or commercial or campaign) simple, dramatic, and memorable?**
- **Does it know to whom it is talking and what it wants to say?**
- **Does it stand on its own without depending on fancy production or celebrity spokespersons?**
- **Does it arouse emotion?**
- **Does it satisfy logic?**
- **Does it have an original idea?**

Well, okay! Come up with one more killer just to be sure.

Stick a couple more good campaigns between those two.

Now you've got a killer sandwich. If you constantly upgrade those merely good campaigns, soon you'll have a killer book.

When you go out looking for a job, you're going to be armed!

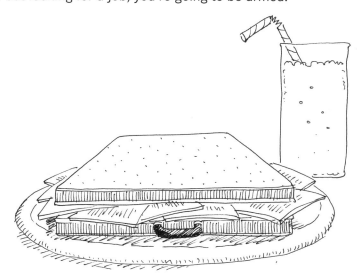

Now you've got a Killer Sandwich!

Q. Why simple?
Simple would put Steven Spielberg out of business.

A. Steven Spielberg's concepts are simple. Stranded extra-terrestrial wants to go home. Man-created dinosaurs run amok.

And Spielberg has hours to tell his story.

You've got seconds.

Your *ideas* should be simple. You can execute your little heart out as long as you don't muddy your message. You're doing ads, you know. And the consumer doesn't want to have to work too hard to figure out what you're trying to sell. Or why he should buy it.

Simple doesn't mean *simple-minded*.

We're not looking for vapid, boring, condescending ads. We mean simple as in pure. Better yet, pure gold.

Your goal is to crystallize a powerful thought in an instant.

I keep saying your ads must communicate quickly.

Think subway poster. You're standing on the platform when the subway comes in and stops before you. The door opens. Read the ad on the opposite side. The door closes. Did you get it?

Or think billboard. You're in your car driving on the freeway. See the billboard? Now it's gone. Did you get it? It pops up on a Web site or crawls at the bottom of your screen. Did it make an impression?

If your visuals take too long to absorb, if your copy doesn't grab, you're going to get some twisted eyebrows and an apologetic "I'm sorry. I just don't get it" at portfolio review time.

James Patterson, former worldwide creative director of J. Walter Thompson and author of innumerable best-selling blockbuster novels, labels these personal, sell-nothing ads we see so much of as "My mind is an interesting place to visit."

Self-indulgent body copy—copy that tells more about you than it does about the product—really turns off the people you're trying to impress.

An acronym from the world of communications: KISS. Keep it simple, stupid. If you have to explain your ad, it's probably a miss.

That's why your ads should be simple.

YOUR BOOK: FORMAT AND EXECUTION

Scott was only months away from graduating from a good portfolio school when I met him. He was prolific and had created some dandy campaigns that were touching and funny. He'd picked products that varied in range from a cigarette (!) to a local shop that sold only electric fans.

And Scott was a very devil with his fine-line Pentel. He could draw like crazy; his products and people were comic, detailed. In fact, I think Scott is a bit of a genius when it comes to drawing.

So, why is it that Scott was hired as a *copywriter* by one of the hot agencies in New York?

Because he's conceptual, he's verbal, and his *design skills*, despite the fact that he can draw well, are quite average.

The line between copywriters and art directors is very blurry. The computer has made it possible for writers to art direct and for art directors to leap tall buildings where once upon a time they had to carry their markers up the stairs. Because writers and art directors are both Mac-fluent, they cross skills. Scott can become a writer, work with an art director, and never miss a beat in his career.

Still, there is a difference between the disciplines.

Art directors: You must have great visual/design sense. You should be able to write headlines. If you like to write copy, that's fine. Present yourself as an art director who can write. Naturally, you must be able to come up with strong advertising ideas.

Nancy Temkin, partner at Greenberg Kirshenbaum in New York, advises art directors:
We want to see books where the concept, the idea, is paid off visually. We look for books where the creator takes risks.
A book full of ads with strong concepts and basically the same layout in each campaign may be okay for a copywriter's book, but not for an art director.
The books that get me to call my clients are the books where the concepts are smart and each ad is a visual treat because it expresses the concept in an unexpected and intelligent way.
It's better to be smart and gutsy (even if some things don't quite work), than smart and safe.

I couldn't agree more.

Copywriters: You must also think visually and you must be deft with the written word, even if none are called for in every campaign you write.

People still read. We still think with words.

As always, the big idea is what counts most of all. If you've got a teammate or teammates in school, you'll work with this partner on visualizing your concepts. If you're working alone, you should be able to create a workable layout on your computer.

As a writer, your goals are big ideas and apt, vivid words. As with art directors, smart and gutsy applies to you as well. Take some risks. Dare to be great. Your headlines are going to have to be terrific—smart, economical, instantly engaging.

In general: Each ad in your campaign should have a new headline. Each word in each headline should be well-chosen.

Grammar and spelling count.

And you really must write body copy. When we look at your book we're hoping to see an impressive use of the English language—fresh writing that makes us think about things in new ways.

In at least one of your campaigns, preferably two or more, write out the first ad completely. The second ad should have a new headline, but might need only a few new lines of copy to reestablish your thought. The third ad might simply have a new headline.

Many areas of the advertising business, including digital advertising, demand superior writing skills in addition to great ideas. Helen Klein Ross explains the ensuing turf wars between print/TV agencies and digital agencies as each one vies to be "King of the Budget." With clients shifting more of their money to digital advertising, including social media outlets, Ross says, "digital agencies are claiming they can be AOR (agency of record) and hand off print and TV to traditional shops, and traditionals are scrambling to realign their departments to look like they're digital."

What do these turf wars mean for you and your copy?

You must be able to write fluently on all platforms, traditional and digital. And writing for a digital platform requires the same skills it's always taken to write killer copy, plus copy must incorporate a social component.

Even if you're destined to spend your career writing nothing longer than 30 seconds, your first writing portfolio ought to have some great examples of your copy "fluency."

Even one terrific long copy ad can make a strong impression.

In sum: A great copy book has big ideas, terrific headlines, well-crafted body copy, and at least one well-developed, long copy ad.

You're a writer. Writers write.

Writers and art directors: When recruiters look at books of both writers and art directors, they're looking to see striking visual solutions—then they'll think the book through again, this time judging your work on the quality and originality of the words and design.

Ninety-five percent of the creative directors and recruiters I polled say they want to see your book on your Web site. They want to be able to look at your work in their own time and at their own speed and download your ads in pdf format.

Your ultimate goal here is to make your entire hard-copy book reader-friendly and easy to handle. It should reflect your level of professionalism and be well produced. Since you are still looking for a job, your book should look fresh and "in progress." Lamination or anything permanent-looking in a mini-book or main book suggests to the reviewer that you're not open to comments or change, that in your mind, your book is finished. And that could prevent them from giving you a critique you may very well need.

In class, in portfolio review, and in real life in advertising:

Be prepared to have your ideas shot down.

Be prepared to do your ads again and again and to come back with something even better.

Q. **How many ads should be in a campaign?**

A. In real life there can be hundreds of ads in each campaign.

For your book, three ads per campaign are generally enough, but it's not a rule.

Two good ads are better than two good ads and one bad ad.

Four or more in a campaign are fine if they are all are really good. The point is to show how your concept is expanded and how your tagline unites the campaign idea.

In truth, the number of ads in a campaign and the number of campaigns in your book aren't the point. *The point has to do with the consistency and quality of your ideas.* Most creative directors like to see that you can expand your campaign into other media; outdoor, Web, out of home, ambient, mobile, etc. This shows that your campaign has "legs."

Be prepared to have your ideas shot down.

Q. How many pieces should I have in my book? Any special order?

A. There's no right answer to this question, but since we're asked this a lot, I'll say your book should contain twenty to thirty pieces that make you proud. That number should probably break down to a book of three or four campaigns—at least three ads per campaign, maybe a few one-shot ideas, and probably some ideas for alternative media that extend one or more of your campaigns.

May I be blunt?

If you can't sell yourself in fifteen ads, fifteen more won't help.

So don't pad your presentation just to bring up the number of pieces.

The order? Just as a good commercial must capture your attention in the first few seconds, so must your book.

Remember that killer sandwich? Whether it's a virtual book or an actual one, put your best ad first. Close with one that's just as good to reinforce that first impression.

Your book should flow.

Let me try to explain what I mean. On one hand, your book is a collection of different campaigns for different products. On the other, your book is one presentation. Your reviewers will be adding up all their feelings about your separate campaigns to come up with a single impression of you.

So try to balance your portfolio with an eye to the whole presentation. Seek a rhythm to the order of your campaigns that feels pleasing to you. Weed out campaigns that do you no good.

Carol Vick, of Kelliher & Vick, puts it nicely, "Keep only the best work. One of the most important things about your book is quickness. Don't ask too much of someone looking at it. Demonstrate that you understand and respect them and their time and they will be much more likely to hire you."

We'll talk about how to edit your book later on.

Too many.

Q. **What kind of alternative media pieces should I include in my book? How many pieces?**

A. Some recruiters want to see what they refer to as "smart thinking," advertising problems that are solved in non-ad or nontraditional ways. Store banners, billboards, bumper stickers, and packaging ideas are all examples of alternative media, and the executions of these non-ads can be thumbnails or brief descriptions of the media, stating the problem and how you've solved it. But the more "finished" pieces, the better, keeping in mind that the idea is key.

Jim Hord, creative director at R/GA, makes a great point when he says, "I want to see a great idea executed in unique ways. Not an idea with a great print campaign and then a bunch of tactics just to show it 'has legs.' Each execution should be compelling enough to make me want to put it up on a wall."

Pippa Seichrist, president of Miami Ad School, told me that at a recent portfolio review seventy agency people came to see twenty student books. The hands-down favorite was a package design campaign by Tracy, a talented young art director, who had created a campaign for Duracell Batteries.

Tracy came up with an environmental approach for Duracell: the notion that old batteries that are sent to landfills are bad for the environment.

Pippa says, "Tracy thought it would be good for Duracell to institute a recycling plan." When their consumer went to a retail store to buy new batteries, they could drop off their old batteries for recycling at the same time. She designed packaging around the batteries to convey this environmental theme. Small watch batteries were packaged to look like a ladybug on a leaf. AA batteries were bubble-wrapped to look like caterpillars, and so on. "Her idea really had legs; it could be spun out into just about any media."

Brian Shembeda, creative director at Leo Burnett, reminds us of the big picture. "The idea is king. The other pieces will fall into place around a great idea. That being said, juniors should take advantage of the fact that they are not constrained by clients, budgets or media buys. I love seeing innovation in any book, not just juniors."

Now more than ever, the idea is king.

Guerrilla Media

The term *guerilla media, guerilla postings*, or simply *guerilla* for short, is now a mainstay in advertising vernacular. Referring to jungle fighters, guerilla media is basically any sort of nontraditional marketing tactic. Or, as Giff Crosby, creative director at M. L. Rogers Agency in New York, puts it, the spirit of guerrilla marketing is to "get the attention of jaded consumers in surprising or fun or new ways, without spending a lot of money."

It's marketing done on the cheap, or almost free, or by not using a traditional paid venue.

According to Crosby, a good example would be Canon's creative campaign in during the 2009 U.S. Open, when it dispatched squadrons of Maria Sharapova look-alikes to the streets of Manhattan, dressed in classic Maria tennis garb, to approach people with free foldout maps to the Open that folded down into the exact size and shape of a new and tiny Canon camera. Now that's guerrilla marketing.

Small companies and creative advertisers have to fight their competition with lower budgets, so while they might not have the cash to dispatch Maria Sharapova look-alikes, they do have posters and paint.

And so in a lot of cities the basic guerilla approach is still postings stenciled on asphalt streets and stuck to the bottoms of beer mugs or the backs of public restroom stalls.

When you're creating a piece of alternative media for your book, you can go with a "one-shot," but if the idea is "campaignable," or if it springs from one of the campaigns already in your book, so much the better. But do keep this in mind: coming up with ideas for alternative media is not a requirement for a killer book.

Bertrand Garbassi, partner and creative director at Publicis, has this to say: "I'd rather see a traditional print book of strong, conceptual advertising ideas than a book filled with lame guerilla ideas."

Giff Crosby agrees. "For a beginner, the most compelling stuff, regardless of what form it takes, is really wonderful ideas, hilarious or delightful writing or a fresh approach to the graphic arts and an original use of the various traditional media. I simply love to see when a beginner shows a talent for noting special things about our culture, or lines that nobody else has noticed. This shows me so much about what this creative person can do for our clients, as opposed to displaying a particular skill in the new media. We know talent can make the leap from conceptual ads to any kind of problem solving."

Q. What about TV commercials?
Should I do storyboards? How many?

A. A *storyboard* (also called a *board*) is a page containing blank spaces in the shape of television screens on which important frames of a proposed commercial are drawn. There's a space beside or below each frame for copy and visual instructions.

Recruiters haven't expected to find storyboards in portfolios in a long time. Most stopped reading them because they were often just an exercise in creating eight frames of pictures with dialogue, and they simply took up space.

In truth, your ideas pop more quickly in print format. Portfolio reviewers can "get" your conceptual ability more quickly in a headline and visual than by reading the dialogue and camera direction on a storyboard.

But. If you feel especially fluent in the television medium, or if one of your campaigns simply demands to be expressed in moving pictures, do one storyboard and make it a great one.

Or, instead of doing an entire storyboard, do what is often called a *key frame* or *key visual.* In this shorthand version of a storyboard, you create only one television frame, but make it big, say half your page. Have it represent the most important instant in your commercial.

The only way a key visual will work well for you is if your idea is a big one, clear enough to be expressed in one frame. Put the dialogue (or monologue) underneath the frame. Unless your commercial shifts location, it should not be necessary for you to describe the visual details and camera action.

Done simply, your key visual will read quickly and show off your television idea to its best advantage.

My advice? Only do a television commercial if it really makes your concept come to life.

Don't forget, it's very important to make your work accessible.

If your campaign is good, people will read the board.

If it's not, they won't.

Keep your book and your Web site free of clutter.

A storyboard represents the important frames
of a proposed TV commercial.

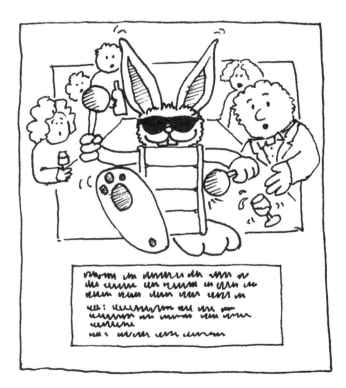

A key visual can work if the idea is a big one.

Q. How about videos? Should I shoot a video to show that I can shoot commercials?

A. As you've heard us say before, the key thing is to have great—everybody with me now—ideas. Doing TV for the sake of doing it will cost you points. If a TV spot will bring your campaign to life, do a board, or shoot a spot with your cell phone, but don't go overboard. No pun intended.

Doing TV just for the sake of doing it will slow your book down and cost you points. But great video ideas produced in a simple, powerful way will knock people out.

Make it great or stick to print.

Q. Should I email a pdf or supply a CD of my work?

A. As of this writing, *most* creative recruiters and creative directors prefer reviewing books electronically when looking to fill a position, and if their Web site doesn't require that you upload a pdf or enter a URL when you apply, you can bet they'll ask for it before calling you in for an interview.

And if you go to a portfolio review, don't have any mini-books to leave behind and have yet to develop a web site, CDs are decent leave-behinds. But since the work is already digital, many recruiters or creative directors will ask you to just e-mail them a pdf of your work instead. It's just as fast and convenient and they won't have to carry anything around with them. Even so, it doesn't hurt to have a few CDs on hand.

Web sites are cheap (or free), cool, and cutting edge; which leads us to the next question.

Q. **Should I develop a Web site to show my portfolio? Are juniors expected to create their own Web site? Or can they hire someone to do it? How many ads should I show?**

A. R/GA's Jim Hord says, "A site is the price of entry these days. I don't necessarily need Flash and stuff flying out at me. I want to know that he or she understands how a site should flow and how to present ideas in an organized way. That said, for art directors, a blog site isn't quite going to cut it."

Kathy Primozic, recruitment manager at Marcus St. Jean in New York, also gives her take on the subject. "Having a Web site is instant gratification for the hiring gatekeepers, creative managers and creative directors. No more carrying or trafficking of bulky portfolios. It enables you to spread a wider net near and far and get a quicker response to your work."

www.youbetyoursweetpatootieyouaregonnaneedawebsite.com

At the moment, a lot of advertising programs don't have Web design as a requirement to graduate, but more and more schools are offering it as an elective, so if you have the option, take it! There is nothing better than saying, "Yes, I did it myself" to as many questions as possible during an interview or portfolio review. I mean, there is no rule that you can't get someone else to do your Web site, but chances are no one is going to do it for free, so save some money and make yourself more valuable at the same time by doing it yourself.

If this isn't an option and you don't have the skills, our friend Kathy Primozic suggests you try one of the many social networking sites (LinkedIn, Facebook, Twitter, Plaxo, Coroflot, Creative Hotlist, etc.), where there is a ready pool of talent that can show you or do it for you.

Still, if you must get someone to create your Web site, put in as much great work as you can to make it your own and make sure that the person creating your site is just doing the production.

And here's another tip: Be considerate of your site viewers and make it easy to navigate. Leo Burnett's Brian Shembeda says, "I've seen too many beautiful and innovative site designs that could not be navigated without an instruction manual."

"Clean is best," says Heidi Ehlers, head of talent attraction and acquisition at blackbagonline.com. And it's not just neatness and navigation you need to consider. "Ixnay on the usicmay. Please. I love the song for about eight seconds, then I can't find the mute button fast enough. Besides. I'm trying to concentrate on your book! It's like someone talking to you when you're trying to read." Same goes for clicking sounds. It's just distracting.

Also keep in mind that some people are looking at your site on a 15" screen, others on a 22" monitor, and using different browsers, so, as Heidi suggests, "Take your site for a test spin" to make sure your work is legible in all environments.

David Baldwin, founder of Baldwin& and former chairman of the One Club, prefers sites that include a downloadable pdf of the work in case it can't be enlarged for easier viewing. If nothing else, at least include a downloadable résumé.

As far as the number of ads, there is no real rule. You can put all of the work that's in your physical book, or even expand it to include other (great) work that you are proud of. The beauty of a Web site is that users have total control of when they want to access it, and how long they want to stay or how deep they want to go.

So if you also do photography and branding, then have three sections, Advertising, Photography, and Branding.

Make it clear what your forté is: art direction, copywriting, etc.

The important thing is to make the Web site your own.

Q. With all this talk of integrated marketing, should my book show campaigns in all media: print, sales promotion, Web sites, interactive, or what?

A. Agency recruiters look at both copy and art portfolios for great ideas expressed in campaigns, whether they be print, guerilla, or integrated.

They assume that great ideas can be translated into any medium, and rightfully so.

Tweeting is now a career opportunity. Who knew?

Q. **We're a team. I wrote his ads. He did my layouts. We collaborated on the ideas. Can we get jobs as a team?**

A. Some agencies are willing to hire teams, but it all depends on what they are in need of at the moment and just how great a team you are. When asked if she prefers to hire teams, headhunter Marie Arteca replied, "It's a yes and no answer—good teams are hard to find but it is always great when you know a team works well together. On the no side—juniors should have the opportunity to work with different partners and sometimes more senior partners."

By the way, should you go on interviews without your teammate for a job that is just for one, make sure you credit your partner or partners for their contribution to the work you are showing in your book.

Your typical art director/writer team:
often, joined at the hip.

Q. **I've been told to write up the strategy statement with the demographic background, etc., and include it with each piece. I hear some agency people don't like to see this kind of thing. What's your opinion?**

A. I'm not a big fan of explaining ads.

When I see these little notes explaining how the product is being positioned and what the strategy is, I don't read them. I want that headline to do the work. And the body copy. And the visual.

If your ads work without the note and you want to keep the notes in anyway—to describe your assignment, for instance—okay. But please excuse me while I play through. I want to see the *ads*.

And while I'm on the subject of demographic background, let me tell you about the sinking feeling I get when a student who has competed in a national competition presents a bound hundred-page "campaign" created by him and his ad club team. This body of work comes complete with marketing data, media plans, and a piece of advertising tailored for every conceivable type of media—from matchbooks to bus posters.

Bethany had one of these books. She was president of her ad club, and her team placed second in the finals. She was justifiably proud of her accomplishment; she'd devoted a good portion of her school year to this effort, and it paid off in lots of acclaim and top grades.

So that means Bethany and her group don't need the kind of portfolios all the rest of you folks need, right? Wrong.

Group work doesn't tell me what I need to know about the candidate's talent and originality. Even if the advertising concept and the executions are great, and fundamentally the work of the presenter, we still don't know who came up with the campaign idea.

Contests such as the AAF Student Competition can be fun and a good learning experience, so do participate if you get the chance.

But don't think you can skip putting your book together. Placing in a national competition is not a substitute for having a portfolio. Period.

Q. **If you're applying for a job as an art director, but you are also a good illustrator and photographer, should you include some of those samples too?**

A. Sure. Easily done on your Web site with tabs to show your illustrations, photographs, and graphic design. But be careful not to weight the book too heavily in a non-advertising direction.

The purpose of putting in more "artistic" work should be to show that you're well-rounded and talented. But don't confuse the issue for folks who simply want to hire an agency art director.

If you're undecided about possible careers, say between art direction and fashion illustration, you absolutely must have two portfolios, two Web sites. You don't ever want to come off as neither fish nor fowl. With two books, you can see two different sets of people and be two different people.

May the best one win.

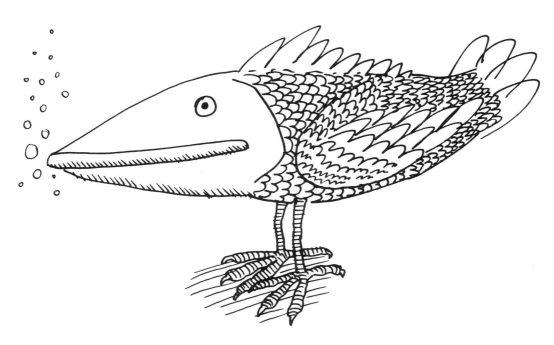

Neither fish nor fowl. If you're interested in two careers,
you must have two portfolios.

Q. I write short stories. Is there a place in my book for them?

A. Just as an art director can put in some design pieces or photographs in his or her main portfolio, a copywriter can add non-advertising writing to their book, but to actually get the work read, you have a better chance if you put creative writing under a tab or link on your Web site.

As longtime recruiter Carol Vick says, "Some creative directors like to see that you have 'creative reach' in nontraditional ways because they want to create nontraditional advertising. Those agencies have been very interested in seeing college-written scripts and short stories."

That said, be careful about using deeply personal poetry as a sample of your work: you might let your interviewer know more than he or she needs to about the love you lost, and college newspaper articles aren't all that humorous to those of us who have long since graduated, so balance your book.

Be careful not to diffuse the image you are trying to present.

You want to be a copywriter.

I do remember one exception to the rule: Mark wrote sound bites for a presidential campaign. This kind of writing has relevance to advertising. It's promoting a "product." The words have to be concise, and they have to communicate fast. Mark told me a thousand lines would bite the dust before one was chosen, and the pressure in this job was intense. Again there is some relevance to advertising.

Was Mark guaranteed a job in advertising because he wrote sound bites? No way.

He still needed a portfolio of great ads.

Q. **I like to invent new product ideas.**
How many of them can I put in my book?

A. Only great ones and, even then, no more than one or two.

Coming up with new product ideas is the least of what a creative person does. It might come up a couple of times in a person's career, but not every day, so developing new products doesn't tell us what we really want to know about you.

Even so, some professors ask you to develop new products as part of your advertising education, and in limited doses this kind of "ideation" can demonstrate an intellectual sparkiness that can be a valuable trait in a creative person.

If you come up with new product ideas, be reasonable.

No magic, please. A tire that lasts forever is magic.

A wallet-sized computer that cooks dinner, diapers your baby, and tapes the hockey game may exist some day, but we're not in the science fiction business.

No fair.

For products you "invent," the technology should be already in existence, or at least feasible. They should be products an advertiser might actually market, that an agency might advertise. Appetite-suppressant chewing gum. Calcium-enriched dog biscuits.

We've seen some new product ideas that were hysterical. A prescription windshield, for instance, so that only the owner could drive his car. Gun-shoes, a sort of a James Bond idea to protect the wearer in the hazardous New York subway system.

However, sometimes a new product idea can be good enough to move your book away from the pack.

Steven came up with an idea for rubber gloves with scouring strips on the fingers and palms so the consumer could really get at those tough scouring jobs: grills, tiles, nasty pots and pans. "Get a Grip on the Grime," said one headline. He called his product "Scrubs. The Helpful Handful."

Which reminds me: it's a good idea to name your product while you're at it. That may make your idea twice as good.

Q. **Should I change my portfolio for different agencies?**
Should I do ads for accounts a specific agency has?

A. No and no.

If you consider each ad in your book as the only ad in your book, and if you are pleased with that representation of you, you will feel confident on each interview.

You'll be able to discuss and defend your work.

You'll be open to good criticism and will be able to pass off criticism that doesn't ring true.

I think you could get into trouble when you put ads in your book that are there for any reason other than showing the best ads you can do.

Say you do a car ad because you're going after a job on a car account. If you don't love the ad for its own sake, you're going to sound weak defending it if it's challenged—and given that experts on the car account will be looking at your ads, you can be sure it will be challenged.

And if that ad is not as good as you can do, it will dilute the quality of the rest of your book.

Doing ads for actual accounts held by the agency you are approaching is an additional problem.

Most agencies have a policy against reading unsolicited ideas for their clients' products. There is, among other things, a danger of lawsuits from people who see ideas similar to ones they dreamed up produced and broadcast.

My advice is: don't deliberately do ads for a specific agency for their accounts.

Q. **I have some produced work that I did during summer jobs. Should I put it in my book?**

A. How good is it? If you want to put work in your book because you're proud of the piece—and you don't have to be there to explain what you had to do with it—then put it in.

If the work is not totally pleasing to you—say it's a couple of cocktail napkins and a menu, and you were heavily supervised—note the summer job on your résumé and forget the work itself.

If a piece of work isn't terrific, just the fact that it has been produced won't get you a nickel.

But your question leads us to another kind of produced work, and that is freelance work.

As with summer jobs, if you do freelance work basically for pay and to the tightly drawn specifications of your client, then the work may not be as good as speculative work you create yourself without heavy supervision.

If your freelance work isn't as good as your spec work, then it, like summer job work, should be excluded from your portfolio or consigned to a special place in your book or on your Web site.

But what if your freelance work is very good? Can it enhance your book? Give you an edge over your competition?

Dany Lennon, a high-profile recruiter and owner of The Creative Register, suggests you go out and solicit freelance accounts for the sole purpose of doing great ads and having them produced.

If your produced work isn't wonderful, just the fact that
it's produced doesn't get you a nickel.

"Forget about money," Dany says. "Go to dry cleaners, retail stores, type shops. Tell the owners you will do ads for them for free if they will run the ads in local papers. Many of these small businesses will be delighted to let you do your best.

"They won't see you as juniors; you'll be advertising people. You'll learn to work with a client, present your work, and get your ads produced virtually as you created them."

Dany backs up her excellent advice with action, by letting juniors do ads for her business. She chooses the best ads, then runs them in award annuals.

Why should you do these ads for free? Because presumably you'll have more say in the creation of the ad.

If your "client" is paying you a fee, he or she may be more inclined to dictate the ad, and you will be obliged to follow directions.

Of course, this doesn't mean you should forget the client's needs and point of view when you're doing the ad gratis. The client will still only run the ad if they like it. Doing the ad for free might give you more creative freedom than you'd have otherwise.

I like this idea, don't you? In a few weeks, you could go from being a starving creative person with a spec book to being a starving creative person with a spec book, produced ads, and a client roster.

Q. How can I make my book sing?

A. Good question.

Because the difference between humming and singing is the difference between being told to keep in touch and having a job created for you.

First, recruiter Heidi Ehler says, "Put your heart into it. All of it. I find there is a direct relationship between how much heart you put into your book, and the amount of heart you put into everything you do."

It's all about "singing," and who wants to listen to a singer without heart? We don't expect to see a portfolio packed with blindingly original ideas. (Most of us have seen so many ideas, don't be surprised if some of your "original" ideas have actually aired.) But one great idea, one killer ad, can be enough to show a recruiter like me that I'm looking at a person who's going to make it.

If you've got one great ad, the rest of your ads should be in second and third place to that great ad, not trailing the pack. And obviously, the more killer ads you have, the closer you are to having a killer book.

And a killer book sings.

When you have a book that sings, you'll have
something very special. A job.

EDITING: WHY AND HOW TO DO IT

Your book is trying to do two things: sell your products and sell the interviewer on you.

As you work to develop a book that sings, believe this: Every ad counts. Here's why:

- **Your judgment of what's good and bad is being evaluated.**
- **We'd also like to know that your talent is pretty consistent, that you've had more than one flukey great idea in your life.**
- **Your book is a presentation. The sum of the parts equals the whole. Do you want a smooth, consistent presentation? Or a choppy one full of question marks?**

Here's how to get good at editing your own book:

Pretend that the most points you can get for your entire portfolio is 100. Divide the number of pieces in your portfolio into 100 and see what each is worth.

If you have twenty ads, each is worth 5 points—even your killer ad.

If you have ten ads, each is worth 10. So, doesn't it pay to reduce the number of pieces to the ones that work very hard for you? I think twelve wonderful ads say better things about you than forty okay ones.

Average campaigns can dilute the effect of your very-good-to-great campaigns. Scripts and storyboards in excess may go unread, and that will cut into your 100 points.

Throw out any ads that have to be explained. Watch out for "punny" headlines, too many celebrity spokespersons, too many non-advertising pieces, too much public service.

Check yourself.

Do you have heartless ads?

Walking strategy statements?

These items don't sing; they moan. Or at least we do.

When organizing your work, put your best ad(s) first, your next best, last. Start with a Pow. End with a Wow. We hope it's not too mushy in between.

Your ads should be clean, neatly presented.

Remember that your Web site will be seen without you, and that means your book has to represent you in the absence of your charming personality.

An unedited book is like a person who talks too much. Boring. That's why you should edit your book.

Q. **What should a book look like physically?**

A. Today, creative people need several books.

To start with, you'll have a main book, or full book, also called the interview book, or your portfolio. This is your *book*—the one that you'll take with you on job interviews: a presentation case or binder filled with great printouts of your ads, and maybe some collateral material in a side pocket. (This might be package design, photography, short stories, or other writings in an enclosed envelope.)

If you like, your interview book may also contain a bunch of your mini-books. As previously noted, minis are the scaled-down version of your main book for you to send ahead or leave behind.

More on minis, shortly.

Your main book should look professional, so please use good taste as your guide. But both the huge, forty-pound suitcase-style portfolio and the zip-up case with flippy glassine pages inside are dated.

Yeah. Sure. Fine. Whatever.

For your main book, copy and art, it's most common to use a presentation book with plastic sleeves or a portfolio such as a screwpost binder. Generally these books are 11"x17" or smaller. They make a nice, clean, professional presentation, and are very easy to flip through.

Take a look at the plastic cases you can find at Sam Flax and other art supply stores, or go online. Pina Zangaro has some really great portfolio cases that you can buy on their Web site. Or you can even go upscale with a burnished metal, wood, or leather case. Frankly, we just saw a book that was covered in camouflage material with red piping and had excellent ads inside.

On the other hand, Carol Vick, owner/creative recruiter at Kelliher & Vick, still prefers boards over pages. "They are more interactive, editable and friendly. You can mount work on lightweight board so it will not be too heavy." Carol also suggests that you open or close your book with your résumé. "Your contact information should be very easy to find and very visible and in more than one place if possible. This applies to your pdf and Web site as well."

Another piece of advice comes from Lauren Slaff, founder and president of Adhouse, a portfolio school in New York, who says, "Art directors and copywriters should print their work in such a way that there is no border around their ads, because the screener's eye will incorporate that border into the layout."

Please just keep in mind that the main point of this case is to keep your ads organized, not to call attention to itself.

Most of the time, you and your main book will stick together.

In the rare instance where you'll have to leave it for review by a creative director, that person most likely will have already seen your mini-book or Web site and heard about you from the creative recruiter, and won't need be wowed by a hand-stitched pigskin portfolio with a hologram of your pitbull on the side.

For best results, put your creativity inside the case, not outside.

But do put a nametag and/or logo on the outside or first page.

Books get lost. With good identification, they get found.

Q. I'm told I should create "a look" with my mini-book. What's cool and what's over the top?

A. First, I should reiterate that mini-books have pretty much been replaced by Web sites (written on your business card or résumé), CDs, and pdfs, which many in the industry now prefer over lugging around lots of mini-books. However, you should still be familiar with them in case your interviewer wants you to leave one behind at a portfolio review. We're in a bit of a transitional period. If your interviewer is over forty, for example, he or she may really like to see your mini-book. Under forty, and they may just find it easier to simply type in your URL on their PDA.

Typically, mini-books are about 8.5" × 11."

They are generally printouts or photocopies of your ads on decent paper stock, sandwiched between two cardboard covers that can be bound at a full-service copy shop with a spiral or rigid or springy-coiled plastic binding.

We've seen some minis that are hole-punched in one corner and fastened with a key-ring clip, and others that are bolted together with rivets. We even saw one that was made of a drapery sample book, an ad pasted to each sheet of fabric.

 The actual cover of your mini-book is an advertising opportunity—more on this when we talk about promotional pieces—but I want to say here that it's good to put your name and/or logo, discipline (art, copy, or team), and phone number somewhere on the front cover or on the first page.

If your mini-book is bigger than 11" × 17", it's not a mini.

If it shrinks to 6" × 8", the person you're hoping to reach may not be able to read the type. According to recruiters, who are your primary audience, the mini-portfolio should fit comfortably on the desk, and the ads inside should be lifesize or close to it.

Michele Daly, Global Creative Talent Director at Y&R Brands, says:
A lot of minis are black, and some have a clear transparent cover so that you can see the résumé that's affixed to the first page.

Some people put a small sticker on the cover, like "Hello, my name is," or a little drawing of themselves, something to "brand" their name into my memory.

Then, when they call to follow up, I associate their names with the little symbol on the book.

I'm looking now at one mini in the stack that has a bright orange cover—it stands out, and I remember it.

That's what branding is all about.

Q. **I just got my BA in Communications and Advertising Design, but my book isn't getting me anywhere. What should I do?**

A. Because of downsizing in the agency business, there are fewer training programs than before, but there are still some really great ones out there. TBWA\Chiat\Day's program is called "Young Guns," and Crispin Porter + Bogusky has an internship program. You just have to keep an eye out and be on top of requirements and deadlines, because with the smaller number of jobs for beginners, the competition is exceedingly fierce.

What else to do?

PORTFOLIO SCHOOLS

These are finishing schools for people who've already graduated, usually with majors in advertising, with portfolios that are not yet of "killer" quality.

**Lots of folks find portfolio schools
very helpful.**

These schools provide a very competitive environment, with instructors who are usually working professionals. The whole purpose of these schools is to help you develop a portfolio that's good enough to get you a job.

And, for the most part, they do what you pay them to do.

There are two reasons these programs work.

First, you focus totally on developing your portfolio.

You don't have the distraction of other courses in school.

In a full-time portfolio program, you are as totally dedicated to doing great work as you'll be after you get that job.

Second, you share this experience with dozens of other young men and women who have exactly the same objective.

It's very competitive, and you learn the kind of work ethic and professional standards you'll need to succeed in the business. When the economy is good, graduates of these two-year programs usually have a pick of jobs.

Some schools of note at the moment are:

Portfolio Center in Atlanta, **800-255-3169**, was one of the first of the "new generation" of portfolio schools. They feature courses in art direction, copywriting, design, illustration, and photography. www.portfoliocenter.com

The Creative Circus, also in Atlanta, **800-728-1590**, specializes in advertising copywriting and art direction. www.creativecircus.com

The Miami Ad School has institutions all over the world; in the U.S., besides the flagship in Miami, there are branches in Minneapolis and San Francisco. It is a unique program with a network of facilities in major ad centers. They also feature courses in Spanish. **800-858-3190** or www.adschool.edu

Virginia Commonwealth University (VCU) in Richmond takes a grad school approach at **VCU Brandcenter.** Students form teams with account executives, writers, art directors, and account planners. Top advertising professionals are on their board. You can find out more about the VCU program by calling **804-828-8384** or **800-311-3341**, or you can go to www. brandcenter.vcu.edu.

Two programs that have been around for a long time are **School of Visual Arts (SVA)** and **Art Center College of Design.**

SVA in New York City has been offering evening courses for years. Many fine people have come out of SVA, and many fine people have taught there. If you're already in New York, you might call their continuing education program at **212-592-2000** or **888-220-5782**. Or go to www.schoolofvisualarts.edu.

On the West Coast, **Art Center College of Design**, in Pasadena, has long had one of the top advertising art direction programs. It is not uncommon for someone from a smaller (and less expensive) art school to finish up at "the Art Center." For more information, call **626-396-2200**. Or go to www.artcenter.edu.

Two other West Coast programs have been around for quite some time. **The Advertising Arts College** in San Diego has grown into **The Art Institute of California/San Diego**, at **858-546-0602**. Their advertising program Web site is www.artinstitutes.edu/sandiego.

In San Francisco, the **Academy of Art College** has a growing advertising program for their growing advertising market. They're at **415-274-2200** or **1-800-544-ARTS**. Or www.academyart.edu.

Other cities have programs—usually of the part-time evening variety. The Boston and Cleveland Ad Clubs have programs. Check with your local ad club to see what's happening in your area.

Chicago has a number of programs. **The Chicago Portfolio School** is at **312-321-9250** or www.chicagoportfolio.com.

Minneapolis has **BrainCo: Minneapolis School of Advertising** at **952-931-0303** or www.braincomsa.com.

And New York now has **Adhouse**, founded by Gary Goldsmith and Lauren Slaff. They're at **212-243-7334** or www.adhousenyc.com.

CMYK magazine, founded by Curtis Clarkson, www.cmykmag.com, features work from most of these programs, as well as *Graphis*, www.graphis.com, so go and take a look around.

If your book isn't ready for prime time, a portfolio school may help you to put your book together and get a job in advertising.

PART II
…AND GET A JOB IN ADVERTISING

RÉSUMÉS

After you've put your book together, it's time to go out there and get that job in advertising.

Naturally, you must have a résumé.

The point of a résumé is to provide a quick summary of what you've learned, what you've done, and what you want to do for a living.

You'll need to bring résumés to portfolio reviews and job interviews, because interviewers like to get a quick fix on your background. If you have an interview event coming up, make sure to bring extra résumés with you; if you are bringing a mini-book to leave behind, paste your résumé on the first or last page.

While a pro is looking at your book and talking to you, he or she might make notes on your résumé and file it for later use.

Make sure your résumé scans easily. Put your name, address, phone number, and e-mail address on the top with the position sought—copywriter or art director—listed prominently.

If you have a Web site—and this is fast becoming a requirement—list your URL here, too.

List your summer jobs even if they're not related to advertising. We know you're not a professional yet, but we're interested in what you've done with yourself up to this point.

Copywriters: We're especially interested in life experience, because we think unusual and enriching experiences increase your writing range.

If you've worked in a psychiatric hospital or on an ocean liner; if you've bagged all-beef patties or driven a cab, tell us. Don't worry if you didn't graduate from college. It's your copy skills that interest us, and if they show, that's what's important.

Art directors: Put all your art education on your résumé, because for you, it's important, but you should resist a common tendency to over-art-direct your résumé.

It would be nice if your summer jobs related to advertising or graphic design. You certainly want to list your computer credentials and any other experiences that we might find interesting.

A clean, distinctive logo of your name is fine, but it must be readable. If you make us untangle your name from the design, your logo will hurt rather than help you.

If you want your résumé to fold and fly like a plane, it damn well better work, or it'll fly right into the trash.

It's a good idea to cite your job objective as the first item on your résumé.

We want to know pretty quickly if you're a copywriter or an art director, and we shouldn't have to figure this out according to what school you went to.

Avoid hyping your job objective. "My goal is to become worldwide creative director" isn't going to impress us. It's the wrong goal.

Kelly's job objective: "What I want out of life: A job as a copywriter and a red Porsche." Okay. A good goal and Kelly's got a sense of humor.

David's objective: "To be the best damned copywriter ever." Way to go, David.

Anonymous's objective: "To use the knowledge that I have acquired from my educational background and job-related experiences to become a success in Art and Advertising Design." I think Anonymous should have pruned out all but the last nine words, don't you?

Your résumé doesn't have to be devoid of personality to qualify as a résumé. Some creative directors I know would like to see résumés with a little spark.

Paul says he had his name printed in big block letters across the top of his résumé. Underneath this huge type in smaller print: "Hoping to be a big-name copywriter."

The résumé can also serve as a mini-book by reducing two or three of your ads and putting them somewhere, usually at the bottom of the page.

Or you might use it as a cover for a few photocopies of your ads.

Here's another idea.

Make copies of your best three ads and staple them to your résumé. No one can object to that, and it saves the creative director to whom you've targeted your appeal a heck of a lot of time. Always appreciated.

Sometimes the small things count: Check your spelling, or better yet, have someone else check it. More than one résumé has been passed on to me with misspelled words gleefully circled in red.

Final note: More times than I can count, I've opened the portfolio of a graduating senior at a portfolio review, looked for a résumé, and not found one. "I've been too busy," he or she says. "I've got finals. And I had to finish my ads."

Okay. But after I've seen the résumés of your forty classmates, how am I going to remember your book? Where am I going to jot down that headline I liked or a note to remind myself that you graduate in December?

If this could be you, and you haven't had a chance to produce your masterpiece résumé, may I suggest you just bang off a simple one on your Mac tonight? Something. Please?

As long as it's neat, it will serve.

Q. **What résumés have you seen that are offbeat and successful?**

A. I'd like to distinguish here between a résumé—a document that's supposed to identify you and your book and summarize your business career—and cover letters and promotional pieces that can be considered advertising. More on this later.

Generally speaking, your résumé should be simple.

Bill, an aspiring art director who had one of the best books I ever saw (we all watched him pick up his gold statues a year later), did his résumé on plain white linen paper.

He put his name and address on the top, centered.

His job objective: "To be an art director."

Following this were his educational credentials, his summer job experience, and awards he'd won at school. He listed references.

The only thing that distinguished this résumé on its face was that the type was set entirely in lowercase. And, of course, the résumé was distinguished by the things the young man had done.

Interviewers got into fistfights over Bill.

Sometimes an offbeat résumé works.

Sometimes it doesn't.

But I know this hasn't convinced you.

So, what résumés have I seen that are offbeat and successful?

The rule here, the thing that makes some offbeat résumés work, is that they demonstrate the individual's talent. They are clever in a way that is directly applicable to the discipline the person wants to pursue—and to the business of advertising.

One of my favorite offbeat résumés belongs to Stephen.

It looked ordinary enough. Stephen put his full name, address, phone numbers, and e-mail address across the top of the page, and adjacent to that the position he desired: copywriter.

Here's what Stephen wrote under the "experience" column.

June–Present

- **Part-time Chauffeur/Word processor for New York consulting firm specializing in nonprofit organizations.**
- **Transport president to and from appointments.**
- **Edit and type staff associates' fundraising proposals.**
- **Deliver and recover Blanche (president's cat) to and from vet.**
- **Claim president's fur from furrier.**
- **Bring in for repair president's pearls.**

June–Feb.—Mr. B_____. New York.

- **Live-in Companion/Cook to 90-year-old man.**
- **Accompanied Mr. B_____ on walks through United Nations Park. Often stopped to see Moon Rock.**
- **Coordinated/prepared Sunday lasagna luncheons.**
- **Initiated subscription to *New York Times* large print edition.**

Sept.–May—New York. Au pair for divorce lawyer and her 12-year-old son.

- **Laundered their dirty clothing.**
- **Washed their filthy dishes.**
- **Cleaned their stinking kitchen.**
- **Prepared their wretched meals.**
- **Never complained once.**

Stephen listed his degrees and his work as a playwright and author, and he ended his résumé with the traditional closing, "References: Available upon request."

So you can't say the above isn't a regulation résumé. But it's an unusual résumé in that it obeys the time-honored rule followed by writers everywhere: "Show, don't tell." And Stephen showed a lot of things. He's funny, literate, and irascible, and he can be creative within a prescribed format.

Loren, an art director, did her résumé in a narrative style.

Her name, address, creative discipline, etc., was in large type, centered at the top of the page. In the same large type, this time in boldface, was this copy:

> **They tell me that to be in advertising I'll need a big ego. The only thing big about me is my hair. They say it's a dog eat dog world. Too bad I'm a vegetarian.**
>
> **All I have is a degree from F_____ University, a faculty award from Portfolio Center, real agency experience, and a vast collection of empty No-Doz boxes.**
>
> **As long as you don't make me brag or eat a dog, I may be just the art director you're looking for.**

This résumé was well-art directed, well-written, shows that Loren has a sense of humor and that she's willing to work all night! I'd ask to see her book. Wouldn't you?

One style of offbeat is the résumé as an ad.

Bruce used this approach. When he was looking for his first job, he drew a simple line drawing on a regular 8.5" by 11" piece of paper of a male figure holding a portfolio. He ran it off on a copier and added some color with markers.

The headline read, "This is an ad for a product that isn't working." In the place for the body copy he gave his name and stated that he was looking for his first job. I thought this offbeat résumé was very effective.

Mia's ad-type résumé was a killer. It was a visual of an Elle MacPherson–type model, soaking wet in her bathing suit. Mia's copy read:

"No way…This is soooo weird. This girl looks just like me. I mean, she could be my twin sister or something. Freak me out! Oh, by the way, my name is Mia. I'm an art director, just graduated from the University of ___. And I'm available."

Her phone number and address followed.

This offbeat résumé worked so well, Mia never got to use it. It was tacked on the wall where Mia was taking her portfolio classes; a creative director walked in, looked at her portfolio, and hired Mia on the spot.

While Mia had planned to send her résumé out to agencies, she also used it as the first ad in her book. Mark and Bruce did the same.

Here's another example of a narrative-style offbeat résumé that began with a phone number, centered at the top of the page.

UPtown 7-3927

I was in the middle of a nightmare when the phone rang. The clock said two-thirty. I reached over and grabbed the receiver.

"Hello."

"Hello, Shelly, this is Bill." The night editor paused. "They caught Son of Sam."

"No kidding."

"You comin' over?"

"Where'd they catch him?"

"Somewhere's in the Bronx."

I got to the paper ten minutes later. I found the assistant editor poring over a picture. "Who is he?" I asked.

"Look for yourself." He handed me the shot and smiled. "Berkowitz. And Breslin thought 'Sam' was a Catholic just because knew how to use a semi-colon."

I walked into my office and turned on the light. The phone number I needed was taped to the wall for emergencies. I was waking the general manager of WCBS-AM to tell him I needed to buy air time for the morning.

"It's the middle of the night," he whispered.

"I'm writing the copy now."

"You want air time for today? What time is it?"

It was four o'clock, but he sold me three spots starting at six. I delivered the script to the station and heard it on the air going home. "Good morning, New York. The nightmare is over…"

My name is Sheldon G_____ and this is my résumé.

I didn't know if this was a résumé or not, but I loved Shelly's writing. I called him in. I wasn't the only one.

Here's one of the responses Shelly received. It was from the late, respected creative director of Karp, Newton, Van Brunt.

949-1318, 949-1326

I was in the middle of a terrible day—two presentations due in two days with a mad account man slavering outside my door, when I got this funny letter.

Demonstrating my inaccurate reading habits, I had to scan it twice before I discovered it was a résumé, not a short story or a misdirected spy note.

When I finally did understand what it was, I fell into a blue funk, a brown study.

I liked it and, I thought, I'd probably like the guy who wrote it.

But I had no job to offer him and no job was looming. I hoped he wouldn't be discouraged and that he would keep in touch with me. But not at 4 AM.

My name is Howard Karp. I am the Creative Director at Karp, Newton, Van Brunt and this is my reply.

Wow. I'm just standing here in the wings clapping.

Here's what Ed McCabe, Creative Hall of Famer and co-founder of Scali McCabe Sloves, has to say about a good, offbeat résumé:

I hired a guy who sent me a résumé, and I was going to hire him even if I didn't like his work when he came in. This guy sent me a résumé called 'A Not-So-Professional Résumé.' And it was about his life experiences and what he had learned. And it was brilliantly written.

And I made up my mind on the spot that I wanted to hire this guy. Because he was communicating about the things that he felt were important and that I also felt were important.

His résumé took me through his jobs as delivery boy, cab driver, parking lot attendant, all qualifications which I think are perfect for the advertising business.

And every one of them had a social, moral, political, or human message involved in his experience in this thing.

And I said this is a guy that is a sponge. He does something that a lot of people might think would be very boring and very dull and he takes the most interesting things out of it, recalls them, and is able to formulate it into a meaningful experience and get me involved in his meaningful experience.

And that is what advertising is all about.

It is taking everything you learn in life, soaking it up, and being able to push a button at the right time and have it come out so that it is meaningful to other people and, just by virtue of its interest and content, turns people on.

HERE ARE SOME OFFBEAT IDEAS THAT DON'T WORK VERY WELL

Wanted Posters

As in "Wanted for Copywriting," complete with a category called "Modus operandi" and one called "Reward."

The last category describes how the agency will be changed forever by hiring this person.

Icky Puns

Icky puns having to do with "new blood."

Icky puns on the person's last name. Carol Flowers decorating her résumé with sweetpeas. Joe Wrench sending a scaled-down model of a you-know what.

Icky puns to the tune of "I'm hungry for this job" or "Food for thought." These résumés are generally accompanied by perishables that putrify in the file cabinet. (Okay, I confess. Occasionally we have been known to eat the brownies and the popcorn, but we don't think we owe you anything for sending it.)

Icky puns that have nothing to do with anything: A sneaker ("I want to get my foot in the door…"). A box of candy ("I'm sweet on _____ Advertising.").

And More

Rap résumés on a CD.

Poetry.

Photos of yourself, especially in your diaper as a child (even then, you knew), studio portraits, life-size blow-ups mounted on styrofoam boards with easel.

Deception of any kind.

To sum up:

Your best bet is to have a great book with a simple résumé inside.

Simple résumés with a few of your printed ads attached work well as a leave-behind after an interview. An abbreviated mini-book, while going out of vogue in favor of a Web site, is still workable as a leave-behind; just make sure your résumé is glued to the inside or back cover of the book.

If you use an offbeat résumé, remember that clichéd, self-aggrandizing, "punny" résumés that try to convince the reader that the creator is talented rarely work.
And lastly:

Résumés that depart from the basic format have to demonstrate your talent in a way that is applicable to the job you will be doing, to the business of advertising.

Show, don't tell.

And by all means, break the rules if you know you can win.

Q. How do you feel about business cards, promotional pieces, stunts, and cover letters?

A. Business cards for juniors are becoming a must-have. One school has been making mailing pieces part of the course work, and business cards are used as part of a self-promotion campaign. The cards can either be left by the individual in an interview or mailed out, attached to a résumé and cover letter.

Create a business card! They're great for handing out
in interviews, elevators, and DMVs.

Also, as we discussed in Part I, students are encouraged to have a Web site, and what better way to always have that URL handy than to have a business card in your wallet, especially if you go to industry events and network. These are activities that turn into a connection that turns into a job.

Most of the business cards I've seen are clever, well-executed, professional.

This one, for instance: "My First Business Card" is in red type across the top of Tony's card. His résumé uses the same font and is headed with "My First Résumé." Both pieces look terrific and Tony has demonstrated that he understands what makes up a campaign.

Vivian's logo is a stick figure of a woman enclosed in a small green field . "Vivian A___ can't draw," says the childlike lettering. Under her logo is her name, and the word, "Copywriter." Contact info follows that. Vivian uses her logo on her résumé and her card, her mini-book and her Web page.

The image is clever, appealing, and makes us want to know more about Vivian.

Scott's business card resembles a snippet torn from a phone book; black type on a white card. Scott's name and address and that he is an art director are in stand-out red.

Francisco's business card had the headline "Carry Your Dreams With You," followed by "Harvard conducted a study in 100 countries and found that regardless of race, age, gender, or status, people who set definable, measurable goals with a timeline and a deadline are 10 times more likely to achieve them. Fill out this card and carry it with you as a reminder."

On the other side he had a space to fill in your goals for today, this week, month, this year, and 5 years, and he signed it with his Web site address. Great way to get me to always carry around his card, and not only am I interacting with it, but maybe he just helped me out.

But I don't want you to get the idea that your business card must have a gimmick, because simple and neat is classic. The most important thing is that the information on the card is correct and easy to read, because the last thing you want is to point someone in the wrong direction.

Promotional Pieces

A promotional piece is a teaser, a send-ahead item or advertisement for yourself, designed to intrigue your target creative director or headhunter and get him or her to go out to your Web site to review your book, or call you in for an interview.

Mini-books were the promotional piece du jour for creative people in the early 2000s, replaced almost overnight by e-mail with a link to the junior creative person's Web site. As e-mail inboxes overflow with requests from job seekers, I can see that for a promotional piece that can be held in one's hand might come back into favor.

If you want to chance creating a mini-book as a promotional piece, here are some guidelines.

You are the product, and the cover of your mini-book can be seen as an opportunity to advertise.

I've seen mini-books tucked inside handmade paper boxes with interesting quotes and text on the lid, and I've seen other mini-book covers that work as ads for their creators. Now that color printers are cheap, it's possible to make up a different mini-book cover for each agency in the world.

Lauren Slaff of AdHouse says, "The mini-book for an art director and for a writer can be different. I was recently very impressed with a writer's mini-book. It was small enough to fit on my desk, yet I didn't have to struggle to read the body copy. Art directors have to be especially careful not to reduce the ads so far down that the message is diminished.

"A mini-book should be clean, self-contained, easy to look at and easy to read. Shoving ten ads on a page so that you need a magnifying glass to read them clearly works against you."

So keep the principle points in mind. The mini-book should be small, light, and cheap enough to get into as many prospective employers' hands as possible, by mail, by drop-off, as a leave-behind at a portfolio review.

A killer ad for yourself on the cover could move your mini to the top of the stack, but smart-looking covers don't have to be more than basic black with a small, clever logo and your name and phone number. Even raw cardboard brown will do. For me, that beats a mini-book dressed in pink bunny fur with sequins every time.

The outside of your mini is much like what to wear when you meet someone for the first time. Make sure this first meeting makes a good impression.

Promotional Pieces from the Advertising History Channel

Once upon a time, before the ubiquitous and handy mini-books and Web sites, some people did send out promotional materials of unique and sometimes questionable value. As with the guidelines for résumés and mini-books, the best promotional pieces are simple, communicative, relevant, and most important, they're good.

Richard Glass (not his real name) sent out glass paperweights with his résumé engraved in miniature on the surface of each. They were fairly nice paperweights as paperweights go, and some people called Richard in for interviews.

Probably out of a sense of obligation. The funny thing about those paperweights was you didn't want one particularly, but you found it hard to give or throw them away.

I suppose if Richard had had a related tag line of some sort, like "Richard Glass really wants to sit on your desk," this item might have made some sense.

As it was, Richard's glass résumé sat around on a few desks for a while as sort of an irritating reminder that someone who could afford to have engraved paperweights made up and shipped was looking for a job. A creative director friend of mine described this promotional idea as "bridging the gap between stupid and 'I'm an aspiring art director.'"

On the other hand entirely is a promotional piece that wowed everyone who saw it—a classic and very effective piece created by Jelly Helm, who has worked at a number of top agencies around the world.

His original promo consisted of a small, shiny black box with this inscription: "I understand the Martin Agency is hiring art directors for $22,000."

Inside the box was an actual check made out to Mike Hughes, the creative director, for $22,000 and the copy line, "When do I start?" Jelly sent five of these personalized promos to the five agencies he wanted to work for. The Martin Agency bit, and Jelly landed his job.

His promo piece also won some awards, and this talented art director became a name in the advertising community before he even began working!

Flinn Dallis, then of Leo Burnett, tells of a promotion that sent her racing for the phone.

> Mary D____ called herself a copy diva. Her mailing piece, business card, and résumé all had the same line: 'The Ad's Not Over 'Til the Copy Sings.' And Mary had a logo of a cartoon opera diva with long curly hair, a horned helmet, breastplate and shield, but in the sword arm was a sharpened pencil. This little character was singing her heart out.
>
> Mary's copy was fantastic. I got her in so fast her curls got straight. We hired Mary in about a minute.

On the other hand, I had to see about two thousand gross and offensive promotions before I saw this one.

One guy actually sent me pieces of his résumé, one piece a week for a few months, with little personal objects in the envelope. Once it was a used razor blade complete with scraps of facial hair. I was scared! I don't even think he knew it. He sent flowers as his finale.

I wish I could just get the kids to understand one thing. We don't want a bunch of junk in the mail. We just want to know they get it.

So. If you're going to spend the time and money on a self-promotion piece, make sure it demonstrates your talent in a relevant way. Okay?

Finally… stunts.

Times have changed, security has tightened and face-to-face time has greatly diminished, so stunts are much less popular now. As a rule, I don't recommend them. Let me say that another way—I strongly don't recommend them. But they are always fun to talk about. Stunts usually involved sneak attacks on a creative director's office. Half the time the applicant was in costume, the point being to get the target to grant an interview and see the portfolio.

Charles did a number of these stunts, none of which worked very well, but he's had a great career, has a sense of humor about himself, and doesn't mind me using him as an example.

It was Christmas time, so Charles rented a Santa Claus suit.

His sneak attack on a small midwestern agency came just before lunch, and the creative director was looking for some distraction.

Rather than bring Charles back to his office, the creative director thought everyone would enjoy the show, so he asked the staff to gather around in the reception area.

Charles, in full Santa regalia, sang this:

"Jingle bells, jingle bells, jingle all the way

I'm a college student who graduates in May

Jingle bells, jingle bells, jingle all the way

Oh, what fun it would be to work here every day."

Feeling a little dumb, but it was too late to stop now, Charles took a present out of his pack; it was a basic résumé and a cover letter:

"Last year I dropped in on hundreds of families, slid down thousands of chimneys and delivered millions of Cabbage Patch dolls. My magical talent deserves better. Please let me put my creative spirit to work with you."

When the laughter stopped and the show was over, Charles got his interview. "I think you need to consider another side of the business," the creative director told him. "Like media or account work."

Undaunted, Charles announced to other receptionists he was from the IRS to see Mr. Creative Director. He got badly chewed out for this one.

He announced he was from Publishers Clearinghouse.

Presumably the creative director was to infer he had won a prize. No applause for this approach, either.

Most of the time Charles got his book seen, but he didn't get a job until he took his energy out of stunt work and put it into his portfolio.

My least favorite stunt was disguised as cover letter and a pair of résumés. When I was with Saatchi & Saatchi, I received a note from CEO Ed Wax on "From the desk of" notepaper with Ed's name printed on the top.

"Maxine, do me a favor," the note read. "There's this great new up-and-coming team. Take a look at their books. The copywriter is _____ and the art director is _____. They're real go-getters. See what you can do for them. I've enclosed their résumés and have asked them to give you a call. They'll really fit in. Please extend them every courtesy and consideration.

Thanks, (signed) Ed."

I was a touch suspicious. Ed didn't have to do this much to get me to see someone. So I called him. And he'd never heard of this wannabe creative team.

Turns out a similar note had gone out to every creative director in the agency (and to creative directors in other agencies, I'm sure). When it was revealed—inevitably—that the memo was a ruse to get interviews, there were some very annoyed creative directors.

I saw one of the lightning bolts that went back to this team, and believe me, it was bad. No interviews from us.

I once witnessed a junior job applicant push through a crowded restaurant and try to insert his portfolio between an advertising luminary and his shrimp cocktail. I've been assailed by bogus messengers, fake telegrams, even a visit from an art director in a wet suit.

It's hard to come up with a stunt idea that's relevant to the job of writer or art director, and although advertising is supposed to feel like it is one person talking to another, it doesn't actually work that way.

I don't recommend stunts. Occasionally, they have worked to get an interview. Most are unprofessional and don't show advertising creative talent. And now, I leave it up to you.

Q: What Goes on in Portfolio Reviews?

A: There are a number of portfolio reviews available to advertising students, including (but not limited to) The One Club, the Art Director's Club, and Portfolio Night (sponsored by ihaveanidea.org). Some of them are open to anyone who registers (and pays), while others are available to a chosen few or members only. Either way, it's good to attend as many as you can. It is great practice for future interviews and you will learn a lot if you're open to serious, non-sugar coated critiques.

Lucy López, who wants to be a copywriter, tells of her experiences at reviews: "When I was given the opportunity to attend ADC's Top 100 Students National Portfolio Review, I was grateful, ecstatic, and gripping my heart before the first reviewer even walked up to my table, but by the end of the night, I had oodles of great advice and just as many business cards. At the One Club's Portfolio Review, I had some really valuable one-on-one time with a handful of reviewers. Both experiences really helped me to improve my work and build my confidence when showing my book."

ORGANIZING THE SEARCH

This getting a job business can be as hard as the job itself. The competition, as you well know, is fierce.

A battle plan is required.

There's a book you should know about—now also available through an online subscription: *The Standard Directory of Advertising Agencies*, commonly called the Red Book (www.redbooks. com). It's a reference book you can use to get a fix on who's who and who their clients are in the agency business.

This book lists every agency in the United States in alphabetical order. It shows their overall size and names their accounts and the officers of the company. There are also regional lists and other useful subgroupings. Many libraries, advertising agencies, and media companies have this book. Find a copy to look through, if you can, and spend some time with it. What you're trying to do is get acquainted with the names of the agencies and what kind of accounts they have.

You can also get a feel for the agencies you want to approach by reading the advertising trade publications. They can provide you with fresh information: Who has picked up new accounts, new creative people hired in key positions, and so on.

These publications can help you get to know the business. (See the back of the book for a full list of resources.)

Advertising Age, published by Crain Communications in Chicago, can be found on some newsstands and is received by agencies all over the country.

Adweek has East Coast, Midwest, and West Coast editions, and they publish a directory of ad agencies.

Some large city newspapers have an advertising column, and if you're in one of those cities, I'm sure you're already reading it.

Finally, there's the Internet. Of course. Most agencies have Web sites. Usually you'll find the Internet is most helpful after you know what you're looking for.

And the next place you should look is . . .

Award Annuals

Check these out. National advertising award annuals are available in most art stores. Find them. Look through them. Go online and check out the archives there. The One Club lets you see them for free, and Communication Arts charges a small fee. Just find a way to see the work.

Which agencies are doing the advertising you admire most? More specifically, what are the names of the people who created your favorite ads? Write to those people. More than one creative person has given extra consideration to a devoted fan.

Most cities have an advertising club and a local advertising awards competition. Many of them also have local annuals, available through the local ad club. It may take a little detective work, but you can track down the people you want to meet. The point here is to create and qualify a list of likely prospects.

Ask yourself: Would you be happy in a mega-agency or would you be more at home in a small one? Find out the difference.

Is location the most important thing? Or will you go anywhere?

Are there only ten agencies you'd work for—and no other will do? Or will you take any job that gets you in?

At some point, you may want to start noting the names of the agencies you like their accounts, and a likely person to approach. That's when the Internet can be helpful. Often an agency's Web site will have the e-mail address of the person to contact.

In selecting your target person, here's a guideline.

In a large agency, you should probably approach a group head, an associate creative director, or a creative director if there are several people in the agency with that title.

That's not to say you shouldn't write to the executive creative director, but he or she will probably forward your résumé to someone else anyway, and it might get deleted along the way.

In a small- to medium-sized agency, you may find that the creative director is accessible to you.

If an agency lists someone as "creative manager" or a similar title, address your inquiry to this person. He or she is often in charge of creative-department hiring and knows in a more comprehensive way where the openings are and when others are likely to occur.

Individual creative directors generally don't have the same overview, and most of them don't have much interest in interviewing unless they have an opening in their specific group.

Once you have your shortlist, you might start calling by phone. This can work in your favor right away because it's quick and it's more personal than the tons of e-mails piling up in the inbox.

Have a conversation with the assistant. Be pleasant and direct. Give your name. Say that you're looking for a job as a whatever. Determine whether there's a job opening, but ask if you can interview, drop off your mini-book, or e-mail your Web site's URL, even if there's no job in sight.

Don't be vague or deceptive.

Specifically, looking for your first job as a copywriter does not qualify as a "personal" call. The fact that you e-mailed your résumé does not mean that the creative director "knows what this is in reference to and is expecting my call."

Q. What's the purpose of a cover letter?

A. A cover letter is like a handshake. If you're sending it by e-mail, it's an electronic handshake. It's a letter meant to intrigue that person so that he or she will want to spend a few minutes on your Web site.

Whether your cover letter is sent by e-mail or snail mail, it should feel as though it's a one-of-a-kind letter to the person who's receiving it.

Don't send form letters.

Your résumé can be one of a hundred thousand, but if you can, create a personal cover letter just for me.

Your cover letter can be brief, and it doesn't have to make me howl with laughter, but it should convey something special about you or, at the very least, convince me to open your Web site in the middle of a hellacious day.

When Marshall Karp was executive vice president of Lowe, he received what he calls "the best letter I ever got. It was from John, a 'starving' writer in Cleveland. It asked me to save his cat, Andy. John had eaten all his other pets, and Andy was next in line. The headline on the cover letter was, 'Are you going to just sit there and let me eat my cat?'

"It was adorably illustrated and masterfully written." And even though there were no openings, Marshall gave John his first job.

You can always write a plain vanilla cover letter:

"I'm an art director looking for my first job. Please look at my book at www. willworkforbreadcrumbsasanartdirector.com and I'll give you a call next Tuesday to see if I can make an appointment."

But, if you're inspired to write a cover letter that works as an ad for you, go for it. Keep it brief and compelling. A good cover letter could pay off big time—even when "we're not hiring."

Your cover letter is a big opportunity.

Q. How long should I wait to follow up a mailing or e-mail with a phone call?

A. Give it at least a week. I know that sounds like forever, but if you can imagine how many interviews recruiters must give every week, even when they're not looking for help, and the torrents of pdfs and URLs that cascade into their inboxes, you'll realize that a week to them is equivalent to a blink of an eye.

If you can get through to a creative manager and make an appointment, great. If your target recruiter won't return your calls and won't return your book, either, this may be simply something you have to accept as a fact of life in this multitasking, hyperventilating experience we call modern life.

Sometimes a kind assistant to the creative manager may be willing to help you by getting you a yes, no, or maybe response to your request for a response to your Web site or mini-book.

And if you get turndowns, take heart, take heart, take heart.

Cathy St. Jean, owner and COO of Marcus St. Jean, a headhunter in New York, says:

"You may be talented, but there are so many people looking for creative jobs right now. You have to be persistent (in a nice way), keep striving to make your book better, keep studying, keeping looking at magazines and refining your taste, and if you really want to be in advertising, keep going.

"Work as a bartender or a waitress until you get your break.

"It's the same as when theatrical people go to Hollywood to try and make it in films.

"If you really believe in yourself, go for it and don't give up."

Ben Thoma, an art director at EuroRSCG, gives similarly inspiring advice. "Know who you are, and what you are good at. And then have a book that demonstrates both. Expect to be rejected. Take with you the comments that help, and keep working—a book is never complete. Don't burn bridges, because it's a very small group of people who do what you do. As Paul Arden so eloquently says in his book of the same title (Phaidon, 2003), 'It's not how good you are, it's how good you want to be.' "

THE JOB INTERVIEW

At last, the opportunity you've been waiting for. An actual meeting with a real person. Possibly you'll get offered a job and have a chance to realize your parents' expectation and justify the $80,000 they spent on your education. Or was it $180,000?

Whew. No wonder you're nervous.

Hot Tips on How to Interview

The clothes you wear to an interview give the reviewer clues as to what kind of person you are and how you'll fit into the agency. I'd leave the taped-up running shoes at home and consider carefully: is this really the day to wear your motorcycle helmet?

Some agencies think khakis and a white oxford-cloth shirt are the minimum acceptable interview wear. Others think the same garments tell the world that you should be in account services!

Says Michele Daly of Y&R, "We want people that have a lot of energy, and sometimes you can see that in their wardrobe. If they're dressed funky, if they're stylish, that works in their favor."

A recruiter I know suggests you research the dress code of the agency where you'll be having your interview and then shoot for the high end of that agency's code. They wear jeans? You wear clean jeans.

Consider carefully: Is this the day to wear
your motorcycle helmet?

If the agency is the height of fashion, by all means, be cool.

But as Betsy Yamazaki, creative manager/partner at Gotham Inc., suggests, "If your nose isn't already pierced, don't do it just for effect. Be your cool self, not someone else's."

Jennifer came in for an interview wearing ripped jeans and her boyfriend's white shirt. "Do you think I ought to have worn a dress?" she asked me halfway through her interview day. I would have said "Yes, why didn't you ask me yesterday?" But instead I noticed that no one who interviewed her that day cared what she was wearing.

One creative director knew she was the right person for his group when she ripped off a piece of cellophane tape from the dispenser and chewed on it. Everyone who saw Jennifer was knocked out by her killer book and her "do advertising or die" attitude, and we offered her a job, ripped jeans and all.

Know where you're going before you leave home.

No kidding, The agency might have moved since their address was posted in that old Red Book you used. Why not check out the address and floor number on their Web site?

Be on time.

You are too low on the totem pole (wait, you're not even on the totem pole) to keep people waiting. Your interviewer has things to do that are more pressing than gazing out the window waiting for you. He or she may not have allowed more than a few minutes for your meeting, and you might miss your appointment altogether.

Or, as my friend Jean-Claude says, "Ten o'clock is one thing. Ten-thirty is a different matter entirely."

Don't be late. Ever.

Be flexible.

One creative director I know can give an interview so fast, you might not know it even happened.

He says, "If you can't take an interview in 30 seconds, you don't belong in a 30-second business."

Some people creative directors or creative people who might be called upon to interview you are sweethearts, especially if they don't interview for a living, and you might be in store for a full-length, hour long, tell-me-all-about-yourself kind of interview plus a tour of the agency. So make sure you've allowed time between interviews if you are doing more than one on a given day.

Be prepared to wait while the person is in a meeting. Sometimes things happen that can't be helped. If you are going to be late for your next appointment, call and say so.

Be prepared for the secretary to come out and say, "Listen, I know you had an appointment, but my boss just can't make it. I'll call you to set up another time." As I said, things happen. Ask if there is someone else who can see you. Can you schedule another appointment now? No? Okay. If you have a business card or résumé with your Web site address on it, leave that. And be nice about the cancellation.

Mind your manners.

Don't chew gum.

Don't smoke.

Don't swear.

Please be nice to administrative assistants.

I had an assistant once who used to come in and tell me whenever someone was rude to her or treated her like a dope.

Rudeness says something about you, and when Dianne worked for me, I got the word. That person you perceive as a stone wall is there for a reason.

Someone wants her there. Or him.

Q. If I were having an interview with you, what would you be looking for?

A. In the first few minutes I'd be gathering some early impressions about you as a person. Do you make good eye contact? How's your handshake? How do you look? Do you seem comfortable or ill at ease? (If the latter, I must try to make you the former.)

Do you have a résumé?

Bring a hard copy. I may want to go over it with you so that you can answer my questions.

Don't worry about being a little nervous.

We expect that, and in a way it's flattering because we know that nervousness means the interview is important to you.

The early impressions I'll be gathering about you are similar to the ones you'll be gathering about me. Do I seem nice to you? Too busy? What's my office like? Will you feel comfortable here?

Will the phones keep ringing and will I answer them? Any ads on the wall? Do you think they're good?

Don't worry. Anything that goes wrong in the first few minutes is retrievable, even if you can't make eye contact because you spilled coffee on your pants. Because when I've opened your book, either your interview book or the one you've posted online, that's when the real interview begins.

I look through a portfolio pretty fast.

Possibly disconcertingly so. I'm on a treasure hunt, and I want the treasure to jump out at me. If it doesn't, I may dig for it on the second pass.

I'm looking for advertising ideas, new ways of looking at the same old things.

Your ideas should make me want to read your ads—buy the products. The more your ideas work on my emotions, the more I like them. And I expect to be intellectually satisfied, too.

I want to be pulled in with a great headline, and see that your copy supports the promise you've made.

I don't truly expect to see a portfolio stuffed full of blindingly original ideas. As long as your work is fairly consistent, one great idea and one killer ad can be enough to show me I'm looking at a winner.

After I'm convinced you're a conceptual thinker, I look at technique.

Are your headlines well crafted?

Is your body copy logical, persuasive, a joy to read?

Are the graphic elements innovative, riveting, tasteful?

If I criticize your work, pause before you leap to defend it. Maybe I just didn't get the point of your campaign even though you made it perfectly clear.

That happens sometimes, in which case you can say, "Did you understand I was using cashmere to indicate luxury?" I'm not afraid to say, "Oh. How stupid of me. I missed that completely."

If, however, I'm having problems with more than that one ad, pay attention. Maybe you're about to learn something. Maybe I can tease out the part of your idea that's good and help you reformulate it into a better idea.

Some reviews of your book will be very thorough. Some won't.

Or. Maybe I'm a complete hack and I don't know what I'm talking about, in which case play along with me just a little. Even hacks have more experience than you have.

Or. Maybe you're resisting improving your book, because you finally got it looking like you wanted it to look, and because it's too close to graduation for you to think about redoing anything, for God's sake!

Hey. Don't lose sight of something important here. *Your portfolio is a means of getting a job. Getting a job is the important thing, not keeping your portfolio intact.* If you are in that last-moment-before-you-graduate panic, and you're getting a lot of "advice," here's what to do ...

Take a deep breath. Now exhale. You don't have to chuck out your entire portfolio just because you've gotten criticism.

Just take out the weakest link: the ad or campaign that took the worst blows.

You know which one that is. Now, start thinking about something better to replace it with. Do a killer ad. Then delete your next weakest campaign. And so on. In this way, you'll still have a book to show and it will keep getting better. *All portfolios are works in progress.* Even professionals are constantly weeding out their books, making them better.

But back to our interview.

Most people hate to give criticism.

It's a lot easier for us to say to a young creative person, "Nice book. I'm afraid we just don't have anything right now" than it is to say, "You know, you seem to be playing it too safe with your layouts." Or "You've really got to work on these headlines. I don't know what you're trying to communicate."

Once we've given this kind of criticism, it behooves us to try to help you, and that's a lot of work. If you are very defensive, you let us right off the hook. Why should we invest our feelings and time if you don't want to know?

And another thing. Try not to take criticism too much to heart.

It's your book that's taking the flack, not you. You're still the same tall, freckled, wacko, sci-fi movie buff, hamster breeder, girlfriend-of-the-boy-next-door you were before you came in for the interview. You're trying to become an even better copywriter or art director.

Guess what? Our goals are the same.

We want you to become better, too.

So. I'd recommend you ask for criticism.

Try to use the interview as a learning experience. The process may seem overwhelming sometimes. So many people and so many conflicting (!) opinions. (More on this later.)

Don't take criticism too much to heart.

Back to the interview once more.

During the interview, I'll be asking you questions. Directly or indirectly, I'm trying to find out several things.

- **What area within the creative department might suit you best?**
- **Are you resilient enough to survive and succeed in advertising?**
- **Are you willing to work hard?**
- **Can you take criticism?**
- **Do you have enough personal confidence to present your ideas and convince others of your point of view?**
- **Do you seem able to get along well with other people?**

Interviewers ask different questions to get at the answers to these and their own particular questions.

One creative director I know wants to know what your parents do for a living. He's trying to discover what might be special in your upbringing that might influence your creativity.

Another creative director wants to know what books you read. And how many. Yet a third creative director is most interested in your feelings about film.

But even though you never know what type of interview you're going to get, creative recruiter Carol Vick suggests, you should at least prepare yourself with the following questions:

1. **Why are you interested in this position and this company?**
2. **What can you contribute?**
3. **Tell me about yourself.**

   Rehearse your answers to the above questions. Do your homework and learn all you can about the company. Because, they may ask you what you most admire from the agency's past work and you don't want to be stuck with a panicky "Uuuhh.... "

But also remember that an interview is a two-way street. You're also allowed to ask questions. Find out who's who in the creative department. How did the creative director get to be king? Every agency is structured a little differently. How will you fit in? What accounts might you work on?

One copy hopeful I know tries to ascertain the interviewer's predisposition to styles of advertising; does he/she hate puns, for instance, or revere elegant prose? If it seems appropriate, this student sometimes asks to see some of the interviewer's ads. All of this helps him sort out the criticism when he's back at home with his book.

Whether your interviewer is a creative department manager, an agency principal, or a person whose name appears in every award book you've ever opened, try not to feel too intimidated. Know how good you are.

An interview is supposed to be a conversation between two people who are trying to find out if they're right for each other. Be friendly and open. Impress me with your personality, but don't talk your head off. I'd like time to ask you about your work, too.

When the interview is over, I'll probably suggest some kind of action: Leave your interview book, call sometime soon, let me see your book again in six months, take some classes to polish up your work, or, perhaps, I'll set up an interview for you with someone else.

If this last step isn't spontaneously happening as you close up your portfolio, you can initiate this closing yourself by nicely asking the interviewer, "What's the next step from here?" Try to get some kind of answer so you know where you stand.

Last thing.

On the way out, say "thank you," even if every moment of the interview was pure hell. And, if you feel so moved, a thank-you note would be appropriate. Carol Vick strongly encourages juniors to write that little note. "This will set you apart from most candidates. Write a separate note to each interviewer; obtain correct name and title spelling from receptionist or secretary. Ask for a business card and give yours in return." An e-mail thank you is also appropriate, but please personalize it and run it through your spell-checker.

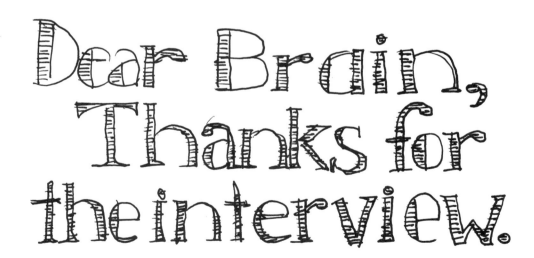

The little things matter. Spell check everything.
(Especially that thank-you note to *Brian*).

Q. **Some people hate my book, some people love it. I'm going crazy. How am I supposed to figure out what to believe?**

A. The most frustrating experience for a beginner is the mixed review. Usually these conflicting opinions are delivered sequentially. You just got a rave from Person A and when Person B sees the same portfolio, he tears it apart.

What's going on here?

Sometimes unusual, very original thinking polarizes people. If some people love your work and you respect these people, and they offer you a job, don't worry about the folks who hate it. Take the job. You can't please everyone, and you don't want to work for people who hate your work.

When a book is great, there's very little disparity of opinion.

For instance, I could like an individual ad, and headhunter Marie Arteca could hate it, *but our opinion of the whole book would probably be very close to the same.*

In most cases, our difference of opinion regarding an individual ad will probably be a personal one. Marie is a ski fanatic. I wouldn't know a ski from a toboggan. So your ad for skiwear just goes by me in my euphoria over your whole book. Marie reads your body copy and she knows you don't know what you're talking about. Or vice versa.

Maybe I think the ad is lousy because I don't get it. She thinks it's great because she does. These simple likes and dislikes are irrelevant when the book is great, and you'll know if your book is great because interviewers, especially the ones who do it for a living, will gush and toss airplane tickets at you.

If your book is terrible, you won't get much criticism.

Most people just don't have the stomach to tell a bright-eyed young thing to get into a different line of work. If you're getting no criticism, and no job offers either, and you've been looking for six months to a year, get tough with your interviewers. Beg us to tell you the truth. We won't enjoy it, but most of us will administer the coup de grâce if we must. (I'll deal with this again later.)

The problem is when some people say they love your work and don't offer you a job. And the people who hate your work don't offer you a job, either. This is what we call a mixed review or the Conflicting Opinion Syndrome.

An average book is the hardest one to critique.

The Conflicting Opinion Syndrome mostly happens with the books that are in the passable to very good range.

What happens is this: the interviewer gets an overall B+ to C- feeling about your book.

Generally, the reason for this lukewarm response is that you turned on your computer too soon (that biggest mistake I mentioned in Part I).

You started with an execution, and your strategy is faulty. So, what we see is something that is almost good or could have been good, but because the ad is misdirected, we get thrown.

Should we tell you to throw out a whole campaign that is fabulous-looking but off-kilter? Or should we praise the art direction and move on?

If we can help you adjust the headline, will that help the ad, or will it just be a slightly better off-kilter ad?

Sometimes your ads are—sorry—boring.

Aah. The old Conflicting Opinion Syndrome.

You understand the whole process and you've figured out some formulas, but the ads just lie there, staring blankly. "There's no news here," I said recently to a copy hopeful. "No news?" she asked, in a tone that could be interpreted as: "Where did this rule come from? I never heard that one before."

Let me explain.

Boring ads are just another form of adlike object.

The ads may be technically correct, but you've told us the same old thing in the same old way.

When your ads are boring we may try to motivate you to shake things up. "Get a little wild and crazy," someone might say.

Someone else might suggest, "Try using fewer words in your headline. This is a little too head-y for me." I might say, "There's no news here."

These remarks sound as though they are addressing different problems. But they're not. The problem is in the work.

We see some problems and potential. We want to explain to you where you've gone wrong, but we're having trouble articulating why that particular ad, campaign, or bunch of ads isn't working, so the feedback we give you collectively may be erratic.

Something about your work is loose and wobbly, and we don't know whether to turn you clockwise or counterclockwise. Maybe either way will work. You get conflicting opinions because I suggest left and Marie suggests right.

We're trying to help.

And believe me, it takes a lot out of us. A full day of interviewing can make me feel as though my blood has been drained by hundreds of little vampire bats. No offense.

Sometimes people have bad days and good days, come from all schools of advertising, all kinds of educational and ethnic groups, and all kinds of disciplines.

I might be offended by something that someone else thinks is a laugh riot. I might pay more attention to your ideas—or lack thereof—and the guy standing next to me (who knows more about art direction than I'll ever know) thinks your layouts are tired.

So you get a thumbs up and a thumbs down.

And we could both be right.

Sometimes this conflict of opinions is based on something as human as this. I'm having a hard time saying, "Yuck, no, phooey," and I want to say, about this one ad at least, "Okay! You've got it here." I want to give you a smidgen of encouragement. And leave it to me, I've just picked the ad that was shredded in your last interview.

This also happens when I've seen your book a couple of times before and it's getting better. But the last guy you saw didn't know that you've improved, so he just sees that average book and he dumps all over it.

Sometimes, in a portfolio review where dozens of books must be reviewed in a couple of hours, the reviewers would like to identify the problem fast enough to help you but can't, so they struggle with what to say.

Their comments may be vague.

Or their attempts to help may be off.

In some cases you may get no comments at all.

I've sometimes felt I can take a book apart in five minutes—even yours. But in that small period of time I can't put you and it back together again. So, I might smile and murmur innocuously rather than start something I can't finish.

Frequently, people who look at books are good advertising people, but not good teachers. While in real life some creative directors are able and willing to nurse you along, many creative directors cannot or will not cosset you.

If you were to bring that heartless ad into your "for real" creative-director boss, he or she could reasonably say, "Where's your idea? I don't see it. Go back and work on this ad again." Or, "This is no good." Period. And then that creative director is going to ask someone else to do the ad. Or do it himself or herself.

Now. Put these creative directors in a portfolio review.

They can't and shouldn't redo your ad for you, and phrasing why a thing is wrong is not their style.

Furthermore, it's not their job.

They are at this portfolio review to pick out one kid to hire.

That's it. And there you are, hoping for the perfect, and above all accurate, critique.

Back to interpreting the mixed review.

When your reviewers mostly agree that your book is very good, you're on the right track. Here's what they say as they look at your ads. "Yes, yes, good, I don't know, okay, good!"

But discounting personal likes and dislikes, reviews that are all over the place mean that you're not there yet.

If you're getting mixed reviews, what should you do?

Listen and learn.

Don't jettison your book after every interview.

Let the advice you've gotten steep a little bit. (I've seen some students take notes for later reference.)

Mull it over. Add up the opinions and then weigh them.

Question your professors and your interviewers. You don't have to accept their advice as law, either.

David had this experience once. He had an idea for a plastic kitchen wrap. To demonstrate that it didn't stick to itself, he ran a sheet of it up a flagpole so that it flapped around in the breeze.

One creative director thought David's approach too esoteric. She felt the only place to demonstrate plastic wrap was in the kitchen. David promptly complied and came up with a kitchen demo for the same product.

Naturally, the next person who saw his book told him the demo was too tame; why didn't he bust some boundaries?

My best advice:

If you hear it over and over again, then it's probably true. Try to understand the criticism so you learn from it.

Then, when you upgrade your portfolio again, you'll be working with your own insight and beginning a process called forming your own judgment.

Your long and happy life in advertising depends upon it.

Q. **When I create an ad, I never think it's an adlike object. I always think I've come up with something that's really good. How can I know the difference before someone shoves it down my throat?**

A. Forming your own judgment isn't easy.

Leora tells about the ad she created for Zippo lighters. Visual: The lighter. Headline: "The Eternal Flame." Without a word, Leora's teacher took out his lighter and turned Leora's layout into warm, gray ash. Leora held up another ad, this one for a brand of men's underwear. Headline: "Eleven Reasons Why You Should Buy Hanes' Underwear."

Leora's teacher took her layout and dropped it out the window. He gave her a cold stare. "Don't do this any more," he said.

Okay, so this was no fun for Leora (although her classmates may have gotten some nervous pleasure out of it), but this is how Leora learned to do ads with heart. In fact, she's lucky, and so are you if you are learning from a tough teacher.

Cultivate the opinion of the person whose
opinion matters most. You.

Making mistakes is how we all learn. So suffer the humiliation because you must. It's part of the process. Go back and read about ads with heart. Check your ads for killerhood. Keep yourself wide open to the learning process so that you'll have a basis for forming your own style and judgment.

And if you want to find out how it worked out for Leora, read her essay in Part III.

Q. Should you go on an interview when there is no job?

A. Absolutely.

There are two kinds of job interviews. One is a job interview for a specific job. There's also a type of interview called an "exploratory" interview where there is no job. You should go on any interview you can get. Because as Leslie Kay of Kay & Black says, "Getting face time is important for feedback! Always encourage folks to meet with you because your personality could really push you through the door even if something is not open...and they will remember you from a meeting more than just from viewing your book."

When creative directors like David Baldwin are willing to chat to help you out, how could you pass up such an opportunity? "There's a limit to my time, but I love helping youngsters out. I remember how hard it was to get to professionals."

Taking exploratory interviews is great practice and a chance to learn. And maybe you can talk or charm somebody into creating a job for you.

Use every opportunity you have to go on a job interview. If your father knows somebody in the business, use that entree. If you're related to someone who is a client of the agency, that's fine. Don't be embarrassed. Everybody does it. Exploit every source you have because it's very tough to get interviews when you're looking for that first job.

By the way, look up the agency before you go on any interview. You'll sound better to us if you know who we are.

It's not clean til it's Nebtar clean.

R. J. "BUD" PLASMOPOD

Personlike organism with adlike object.

Now, let's say you've had a great interview and there are no openings, but you think the interviewer genuinely likes you. That's your cue to say, "I really want to get into advertising, and I'd love to work here. Do you know someone who's looking for a junior writer at some other agency or someone who'll see me even if they aren't looking?" People have been known to give out a list of names. Lisa, a junior art director, parlayed two names into thirty before she was hired—just by asking that question.

Q. **If you have a decent book, but you're not a salesperson, will you have less of a chance getting a job than the good salesperson with the bad book?**

A. I won't say personality doesn't count. It can and does. But let's not conclude so quickly that you don't have one.

If you have a very good book, not just a decent one, someone will hire you for your talent.

A great part of salesmanship is *confidence*, and once you've been hired for your talent, the confidence should come. Sales is the whole point of advertising, but you don't have to be a razzle-dazzle presenter to get a job and to succeed.

I've never even heard of someone with a good personality being hired with a bad book. Lose no more sleep over this.

No contest.

Q. When I'm asked to leave my book, should I do it? How long must I leave it?

A. When you're asked to leave your main book, it generally means that your mini-book or Web site has gotten high marks by the creative manager or someone else in the agency, things are heating up, and you're being actively considered for a job. Good for you!

You shouldn't allow an agency to tie up your interview book for an unreasonable length of time. But be fair. Don't expect someone to look at your book right away.

When you leave your book, ask how long they're likely to keep it. Give them a week if they need it that long, more if it's a real job and you're in the running.

Some kids we know have *two* main books, so that they'll have a spare if they are up for two job interviews at the same time.

When you have to pick up your book, give the agency a heads-up the day before. Then call again as a reminder on the morning you're coming to get it.

This way, your book won't be locked in a closet when you arrive, and the person who has been keeping your book knows that it is "active." In most cases, if he or she hasn't seen it yet, they'll do it right away.

How long is too long for an agency to hold onto
your book? That depends...

By the way, make sure you have your name somewhere on or inside your portfolio. It's not even a bad idea to put your name on the back of each ad, just in case.

Q. If you know you've got spark, how do you make a dumb, inanimate portfolio reflect the wonderfulness that is you?

A. Sorry. If it's not in the book, the wonderfulness that is you will have to be applied to some other profession. Or, don't give up until you've learned how to make the transfusion from you to it. Your question makes me think you can do it.

Q. When the person across from you says, "I really like your book, but there aren't any openings right now. Keep in touch because that could change," does that mean keep in touch or something else?

A. It means keep in touch. But don't be a pest. Figure out how to be persistent in a pleasant way. Ask if you can keep in touch via e-mail—it's not as intrusive as the telephone. Take your cues from the interviewer. If he or she calls you back to see how you're doing, the invitation was quite sincere.

Ditto if an encouraging message is relayed from the interviewer to the assistant to you. If the assistant is pleasant to you when you call, ask her if a call from you to check in every three or four weeks would be okay with her. Perhaps you might send a note (or e-mail?) every now and then with a new (pdf?) ad attached.

Don't call your target at home. Don't drop by unannounced.

If you follow up with me in six months, please don't act like I loved your book if I didn't actually tell you I loved it. If I really loved it, I'll remember you, and if I didn't, I'll look you up in my database where I noted exactly what was in your book and exactly what I thought.

And do keep working on your book so that if you get another appointment, your book will be even better than before.

Q. Are interviewers willing to see you and your book again?

A. Everyone is different, but let's be optimistic. Let's not assume that you had your one chance with Cliff Freeman or Gary Goldsmith (or insert your hero's name here) and that was it.

Call and ask if you can send a pdf of your latest ad or a link to your site once you have made some updates. If enough time has elapsed for improvement to be plausible, I'll bet three out of four people will say, "Okay, you can show your work again."

But this question leads me to an important point. When you start approaching the people on your list of prospects, you should launch your attack in "flights" of four or five agencies.

Then, stop and analyze the results.

Did your book result in any interviews or encouragement? If not, you could send out another flight, or take this opportunity to redo your book before sending it out again.

Pull a questionable campaign and replace it with a better one.

Reorganize. Rethink. Rewrite. Redesign.

It's okay to stop and regroup before charging ahead again.

Q. Is it helpful to go to a headhunter in the advertising field, or should I just go directly to the advertising agencies?

A. An employment agent can help you—maybe. If they're impressed with your book, great, they'll try to place you. They'll occasionally call personal friends and will sometimes waive their fee to the ad agency if a job is created for you, just for the satisfaction of getting you a first job and in the hope that when you're looking for your second job, you'll call them.

But if an agent doesn't fall in love with your book, you may not get an interview. No interview, no feedback.

You also have to understand that employment agencies don't get many requests for juniors. Most advertising agencies are deluged with requests from beginners looking for job opportunities and don't want to pay a fee for someone they can hire for free.

Also, it takes time for an agent to place a junior, and they don't have the time to work with and develop all the juniors who call them.

A friend at a placement agency in New York: "I have a number of clients who every so often ask, 'Have you seen any great juniors?' When that happens, I'm delighted to send along a few exceptional people. But they do have to be exceptional."

That response is the rule rather than the exception for most employment agents, although some individuals and a rare agency do more work with juniors than others.

Check with your peers or last year's graduates. They may know of some kindly headhunter who loves juniors and would love to see you.

HOW YOU FIT INTO THE PICTURE

I would think it must be difficult from where you're sitting to imagine how you'll fit in and function in an advertising agency.

You know that life in a company is bound to be different than life in school. And you're right.

Because in the real world advertising is a collaborative effort, you'll find that ad-making is no longer solely concentrated on you and your idea.

You'll have a teammate with his or her individual point of view, supervisors in layers above you with their points of view, layers of account people with their points of view, and strategies developed when you were nowhere around.

And there will be a client—actually the "client" may be dozens of people with varying objectives, personality, biases.

There will also be market research testing, the results of which may alter your brilliant ideas. And there will be air dates and executional restrictions of all kinds.

The good news is: you'll never be alone on a project again.

When you get that job, you'll be joining a team.

You'll have backup, support, leadership, and resources to tap into beyond your imagining.

And there will be people who will be depending on you.

Excited? I would be, too.

Q. How are creative groups organized? Do you have one teammate on every project or do you get changed around?

A. The basic organization chart looks like a pyramid.

There's a creative director at the top of the heap, a small clutch of supervisors below the creative director, and a bunch of copy and art folks under each supervisor.

The size of the agency and capacities of the creative directors determine the dimensions of the creative group. And, naturally, titles and responsibilities vary from agency to agency.

Generally, the creative director is responsible for all the people and the advertising on his or her accounts in his or her division.

The supervisor-types below the creative director are responsible for the work on their accounts, with less responsibility for people management.

Copy and art people are responsible for the assignments they've been given.

In some organizations, you could work with one teammate on one account, another teammate on a different account. In some agencies, you two are joined at the hip until otherwise informed. Sometimes one or the other of you might be asked to help out on a piece of business in another creative group, for or with another person.

Q. **What kind of beginning jobs are there for art directors and writers?**

A. With increasing competition, college grads are taking internships or freelance jobs with hopes of being hired full-time after it's over. Agencies feel more confident in hiring you because they know they like you and know your work ethic.

There are also junior-level openings if you are lucky enough to get one right off the bat. Just keep in mind that unfortunately "the days of mentoring juniors is pretty much gone," as headhunter Nancy Temkin points out. "Juniors now come into agencies and need to hit the deck running. Used to be that they would cut their teeth on projects, learn the craft as they went. Now they are handed a major brief the minute they walk in the door."

And, it's more and more common now for junior creatives to get hired and find themselves in the thick of a major advertising push on day one, work on a Web site on day two, so please bring your computer skills to the party. Everything's electronic.

EuroRSCG's Ben Thoma says, "Expect to be asked to be involved in Social Media as well. Most older folks in the business look to the younger crowd for guidance in emerging medias and technologies."

Young creatives paired with each other, or with someone slightly more senior, are soon working on their own ads, sometimes their own accounts, coming up with ideas, not only assisting other people with their ideas.

Q. What is a day in the life of a junior like?

A. In your first job, no matter what it might be, you can impress people by demonstrating your untiring energy and your desire to learn. Try to get someone who's involved in TV to let you tag along to an after-hours recording or editing session. (Many of these sessions go on late into the night and over the weekend.)

Volunteer to help other team members in a crunch. Creative directors would rather you come to them than have to go looking for you.

Make yourself someone who can be counted on. Volunteer and make sure to follow through. I'm not talking brownie points here. I'm talking about putting yourself in a position to learn so that you can contribute sooner, give a lot back, and in the process get to more of the places you want to go.

It's impossible to overstate how much good you will do your future if you work extra hard at this time in your career.

Q. What's a typical working environment like? Lots of open offices? Working in groups? Fairly informal?

A. It could be a Dilbert cubicle, an office with a door, or even an office with a window. The Virtual Office may be coming, and many top freelancers may be able to create their own unique work situations, but for your first few jobs, you pretty much have to take whatever they happen to have. Now, most agencies are fairly informal. "Casual Day" now lasts all week, except for the occasional presentation.

Work extra hard at this time in your career.

Q. Should I care how much my first job pays?

A. I wouldn't. If you're getting lots of bites from agencies of relative merit, and you like the people who want you equally, then by all means go for the most money. If, however, you get more offers from other agencies—one of which might prove more fruitful for your career than the other—disregard the money and take the job with the most growth and learning opportunity. You'll make up the dollar difference some other year, and by then a couple of thousand dollars one way or the other won't make a difference. (See Doreen Dvorin's essay on salary negotiation in Part III.)

Q. If the agency that offered me the job wants me to relocate, who should pay the expenses?

A. The general rule on this is based on who made the approach. If you go out to San Francisco and knock on doors and land a job, you'll probably be asked to pick up your own moving expenses.

If, however, you are going to school in Atlanta, and a recruiter comes to your school from San Francisco, they may be prepared to pay for your relocation. But don't count on it.

Some protocol:

If you are flown in for an interview, fly coach. Don't pig out on champagne and oysters via room service and charge the agency. Don't take the subway and charge the agency for a cab.

If you want to take the subway, take it. If you want to take a cab, take that. Don't fly out on Friday and expect the agency to pick up the tab for your weekend.

Good manners would dictate that you fly home Friday night, or if it's a cross-country journey, the following morning.

If you want to spend the weekend in a city you've never seen before, do so, but at your own expense. Or stay with a friend.

But don't cheat, and don't take advantage.

It's okay to set up interviews for yourself with other agencies since you happen to be in town, but don't flaunt it. And make the schedule of the agency that is paying your way your top priority.

If you end up getting an offer from someone else, you really owe it to the agency that flew you in to tell them. Don't expect that agency to be pleased, but if you don't want an enemy for life, do give them the courtesy of telling them about your offer, and a chance to match it.

If you get an offer from the agency that paid your expenses, but don't wish to take it, be extra gracious when you turn them down. Flowers. Notes of appreciation. You get the drift.

In closing, any time an agency pays your expenses, whether it's for interview purposes or a relocation, save your receipts. No padding. Ever. Promise?

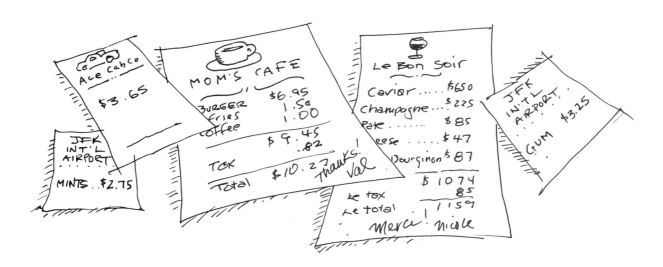

No padding your expense account. Ever.

Q. Does it make sense to take an administrative job if there are no copywriter jobs right away?

A. Yes, it can make lots of sense. It's probably better for you to be an assistant in an advertising agency, especially if you are an assistant in the creative department, than to drive a cab or waitress at a diner (although people from both of these professions have done very well in advertising).

You'll be exposed to people in the business. You'll hear the way they talk about their work, and you'll become familiar with the process of doing advertising and with the experience of working in a company. And, you'll make friends who can help you with your book.

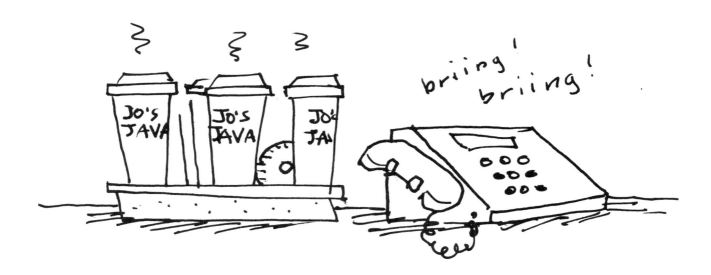

Coffee to be fetched...phones to be answered...it's a start.

And remember, as longtime creative recruiter Carol Vick says, "It is much easier to get your second job than your first. After six months you should consider taking a job that might not be your first pick. If you stay in the search for a very long time it may give potential employers the idea that there is something amiss. There are good jobs in strange places and one of these jobs just might be the right one for you. You need a place where you have a creative mentor and an opportunity to build your book."

Often assistants are given a chance to write some copy or design a free-standing insert, and many are promoted.

Carin, formerly a creative assistant, now a creative supervisor, offers this advice on "how to climb out of the secretarial pool." She says:

> You've literally got to advertise. Tell the people you work for that you want to be a copywriter and beg for assignments. Take copywriting courses and ask your bosses to critique your book. Set your goal and work toward it with perseverance.
> If you just sit around waiting for some group head to read your mind and magically drop a coupon assignment on your desk, you could end up waiting an awfully long time.

John was a studio assistant who asked for an opportunity to work as an art director in the agency's hottest group, and he got his chance. He knew this opportunity would be pass/fail and if he didn't make his mark he would be out of work pretty fast.

John had a wife and child, but he took the risk.

Today, that risk has paid off in a superior reel of commercials, a vice presidency, and a long row of metal statues on his window sill.

Laura was an assistant in creative management. She also answered telephones for seven television producers. Laura went to school at night, worked on her book, and was promoted to junior copywriter within a year.

Two years later, Laura has a fat book of produced ads, a few good pay hikes, and has gone on location to the Far East.

The business is filled with people who have stories like these to tell. But remember, the job you are being paid to do must be done diligently and with a good attitude.

What the "boss" really wants is an assistant who does the job he or she was hired to do. They don't want someone who is above getting the coffee or who makes it all too obvious to others in the assisting tier that they are just "passing through."

This kind of attitude can be very disruptive, and it devalues jobs that are necessary to keep an agency running smoothly.

For these and other reasons, don't expect every boss to be patient with a hopeful creative person's ambitions, especially if that person is forgetful, sullen or—how shall I put this—a little distracted.

My advice

If you can't get a copy or art job right away, take an agency job that's not copy or art if one is offered.

Do your "crummy" job very well. Make friends.

Make your boss want to offer you a good reference should you need it later. Work on your book on your own time. And when it's good enough, try to get a promotion. If you can't get promoted, try to get a job in another agency.

Q. I'm a writer in my thirties. Am I going to have trouble breaking in as a junior?

A. I think you'll be pleasantly surprised to hear this. No problem.

Creative people aren't too particular about things like age, background, or education. They only care about how good you are at what you do. Your age may even act in your favor.

After a year or two of junior-level work, people may simply see a thirty-year-old writer and forget that, in terms of experience, you're just a "kid." After all, you have the poise and sophistication most twenty-three-year-olds haven't yet acquired.

After a career as a waiter in some of New York's best restaurants, Ray got his first copy job at the age of thirty-four. I don't think I'll ever forget the look on his face when a creative group head, who started working at the agency a week after Ray started his first job, handed him and his art director a full-sized assignment. She never questioned Ray's length of time in the business, she just gave him a deadline.

A week earlier, Ray had been standing in front of customers reciting the specials of the day! After a few moments of sputtering, he jumped right in. Jumping right in is kind of a trademark of Ray's, and he's considered a very valuable member of the agency team.

So, if your cap and gown went into mothballs long ago, or if you never graduated, don't worry. In fact, you may find that you'll get raises faster than your younger associates because your superiors recognize and reward your maturity.

Q. When do you get to do television commercials?

A. It depends on the size of the agency, the accounts and the luck of the draw. Could be immediately; could be in two years.

The larger packaged goods agencies, the ones who do 80 percent or more of their work in television, are more likely to let you do a commercial sooner than a small agency that only does a few commercials a year.

In a large agency, you could find yourself coming up with a TV idea for an account before you get your I.D. card from personnel. You may or may not get to go on the shoot if the commercial is approved, but you'll get your name on it, and you'll feel great.

In a small agency, it's more likely the top teams are going to do all the television, but you may get a stronger grounding in print than your large agency counterparts.

Whatever the size of the agency you join, you can prepare for the time when you will do TV by learning as much as you can about the process. Ask to go on local shoots. See if you can attach yourself to a producer or two when your schedule and theirs permit. Many shoots and recording sessions go on at night.

If you find yourself in a job where the prospects of ever doing television are close to zero, learn what you can, and then, unless you've decided on a career in print, consider finding another job.

You may get to do television in a couple of years.

Q. Can you tell me what my career and salary objectives should be?

A. Your first five years should be spent working hard at learning your craft and working with as many good creative people as you can. Your starting job could pay from an average of $30,000 to $45,000 depending on the city, the state of the job market, and how fabulous your book is. Star hires from portfolio schools may get much more.

After that, anything goes. You could be making six figures with lots of perks, or you could wash out of the business.

Many people would tell you that this is not the stuff you should be worrying about right now; that you should be worrying about learning, growing, coming up with big ideas that become successful and even award-winning campaigns.

You know something? They're right.

Q. Is advertising really as fast-paced, life-on-the-razor's-edge, laugh-in-the-face-of-death job that I've always heard it was? Is there a high stress factor? Why do they call it a cutthroat business?

A. There are some aspects of the business which may seem a little cutthroat. For example, advertising agencies are suppliers to their advertiser clients; if the agency gets fired, so can you—whether you did anything to deserve it or not. One reason advertising people make so much money is to offset this risk.

Competition is the essence of advertising. It's one of the ways businesses compete in the marketplace. Suppliers compete for jobs with agencies, creative groups in agencies often compete against each other, and agencies compete against one another to pitch accounts or to keep them.

The result of all that competitiveness seems to result in a tough, straightforward, to-the-point attitude, to the effect that people in advertising work harder to cut through the b.s. than they do to cut anyone's throat.

Advertising is a business that seems to work well for nimble people. The quick, the bright, those who are adept at walking on quicksand can make big money at a fairly young age—so advertising does encourage a certain amount of aggressiveness and self-promotion.

I've also noticed that the young people who acquire additional skills—such as the ability to make presentations, for instance, or those who get into television right away—can move ahead rather quickly. And so this doesn't go unsaid, great ads are like money in the bank. Those "kids" who have genuine talent are in demand and will always be in demand.

The more you dig in and learn, the better the quality of the work you do, the more useful you are to the people you report to, the sooner they can send you out to a meeting or a print shoot without them, the more appreciated you will be.

I'm talking about legitimate skills acquired by hard work, now. Buttering up bosses will earn you antagonism from your peers and may catch up with you later.

Bluffing your way in over your head could be a learning experience, or it could cost your agency thousands in ruined film footage, excess talent fees, or even lawsuits. In some agencies you might get forgiven once. In others, it's back to you and your book. And the street.

As for stress, I won't say that good creative people thrive on stress. But I won't say they don't.

I won't say that good creative people thrive
on stress. But I won't say they don't.

My advice:

Work hard. Do good. Put the team's interests before yours. And—this is not a contradiction—keep your eye on your career. Those "kids" who have the earmarks of potential leaders are watched by those in a position to make it happen.

Promoting from within is desirable in all phases of American business, not just advertising. Advertising is simply a faster track than many businesses.

So don't let this talk of bloodletting scare you off. If you get into advertising, you'll make friends that will last a lifetime. You'll have fun. You'll mingle with smart people who will mingle with you because you're smart. You'll be in a field that is quite small and quite hard to crack—and you got in! You'll be able to show the fruits of your labors to your friends and your children.

And, if you know your job and do it well, you can have a long and rewarding career.

Q. I'm in my junior year at school. I have an offer to drop out now and take a job with a good local agency. Should I get my degree, or should I take the job?

A. Are you enthusiastic about the job? Will your parents kill you if you don't get your degree? Sorry to ask questions, but there are many factors involved here.

If you're good enough to get a job offer before you graduate, I don't think this job offer will be the last you'll ever get. In fact, these exact people might offer you a job again when you graduate.

If you're close to that degree that your parents have been paying for, why not finish what you started? If you're working nights to pay for that last year of art school, getting a good job is why you went to school and you don't need to graduate.

Either way, as far as your résumé is concerned, your degree doesn't mean a whole lot to us. I mean, it could be interesting if you get a degree in law from Columbia, but, as I've said two hundred times before, what we care about is your book.

Q. How much bearing does one's GPA have on hiring? Can a wonderful book make up for a less than wonderful GPA? Can coming out of a good school give me an edge?

A. The best schools are making sure their copy graduates can think visually and their art graduates can think verbally. These ambidextrous creative people can have very sharp-looking books.

The schools that consistently turn out graduates who have great books get the most attention from the agencies. And in this way, coming out of a good school can give you an edge. But only in this way. Your diploma is not a license to get a job.

We don't care about your grade point average.

We care about your book.

Q. **What's expected of a first year employee? What are the major reasons that juniors fail?**

A. Junior-level creative people are expected to show up earlier and stay later than anyone. Be willing to do any kind of work. Learn, learn, learn.

And Neil Raphan, senior vice president and associate creative director at Saatchi & Saatchi New York, agrees. "Once someone gets a job they should be constantly asking for more work. Never say you're too busy. Be excited about any assignment you get. You are your own apprentice. Grab the experience."

Failing in the first year is hard to do, but here's how to do it:

- **Bad-mouth other people's work.**

  Especially if you're not so hot yet yourself.

- **Act like you're too good to work on certain assignments.**

  Make faces, roll your eyes, and throw deep sighs.

- **Be lazy.**

  Hide when your supervisor comes looking for you or make your supervisor nag you to get assignments finished on schedule.

One surefire way to fail in your first year on the job:
Hiding from your supervisor.

- **Contradict your boss in a client meeting.**
- **Keep coming back with that same old ad your boss has killed.**

(You know it's great even if he doesn't get it.)

- **Play big-shot with a supplier.**

Do this especially if it looks like there's something shady going on, like kickbacks, or favors, like producing ads for your book in exchange for giving the supplier a job, etc.

- **Don't live up to the promise in your book.**

As in, did you really do those spec ads? Yes, this happens. And, sad to say, it happens at many levels, from beginner to longtimer.

If you lift someone else's ads and are found out, you will find this is one area where retribution is swift. No agency wants a thief in their house. Period.

Actually, hardly any people lose their job in their first year except for reasons that are outside their control.

Namely, the agency has a cutback and the extra junior art director is seen as an unaffordable luxury.

If you should happen to lose your job because you made some mistakes, own up and learn from them.

If you lose your job because of agency finances, there is no stigma attached, believe me. And you now have an edge on all those inexperienced people looking for their first job.

Q. How long a commitment does an agency expect from you?

A. Two to three years sounds about right. But I'd still call that a minimum.

If you're doing well and are appreciated, why leave? If you hit a rough patch, before you bail out, talk to someone who's in a position to make things better for you and see if they can. A good rule of thumb is to stay at an agency long enough to get the most from the experience that you can in order to expand your network and range, and move on.

If you've jumped around a lot, be prepared to explain why.

Q. Is it better to be a small fish in a big pond? Or stay in a small pond until I learn how to swim? Or should I go to NYC?

A. I guess I'd advise you to determine which is more important.

A career in the big time? Or a good job in your home state?

One thing does not lead to the other, nor does it necessarily obstruct it. If you like Santa Fe, don't force yourself to go to New York. If you think you'd like the intensity of the big city, go for it now.

Two years in an agency in Santa Fe isn't going to help you get a job by itself. But what will help you get a job in New York is if you did very good ads in Santa Fe. Otherwise, you'll have to rely on your spec book.

You won't quite be going back to zero, but you won't quite be in the same place as someone else who's been getting good work produced during his or her first two years.

A little fish in a little pond with a view.

Q. Is it true New York is no longer the center of advertising?

A. The center of advertising has been a moving target for years. Chicago, Minneapolis, Dallas, San Francisco, Los Angeles and other cities have long been featured in the advertising news of the world. Richmond, Portland, and Austin are also homes to agencies with national stature.

These days, you don't have to work in the Big Apple to make it, and right now the odds of getting a job in New York are tougher than ever. Headhunters and creative managers suggest that you take a job offer wherever you find it, and if your heart is set on New York, send out your mini-book again at a later time.

And, by the way, New York City isn't everyone's idea of fun. Don't move to New York unless you've really checked out what it's like to live there.

You might be happier being a star in Dallas instead.

Today, if you can make it in Portland, you can make it anywhere.

Q. **What are the odds of survival for a single, unemployed male with no friends or contacts who just happens to show up in New York?**

A. A lot depends on how flexible you are about the kind of work you may have to do until you get an agency job. And are you willing to live with someone or some two or three until you can afford a decent apartment?

You might not be able to afford Manhattan. For years, Steve, Rick, and Brian tripled up out by the airport in Queens.

Before you pack your trunk, sell your car, and kiss your sweetheart goodbye, try to pave the way. Make calls, send letters to schedule appointments. Do a two-week foray before you move.

Network around a little. Who do you know who knows someone living in New York? Are there any friends from school who might let you sleep on their floor for a few weeks? Or friends of friends?

Now, take a trip. See how things go. See if you even like New York. If you do, and if your interviews have given you reason to hope, get a fix on the housing and interim job markets while you are in town. In a two-week, pre-move visit, your status can be altered from friendless, contactless, unemployed male to unemployed person with friends, a bed, and prospects.

Maybe you've got friends in New York who'll let you
sleep on their floor for a while.

Q. **What about internships? What are they about?**
And how can I get one?

A. Agencies of all sizes hire interns.

Sometimes there is a formal training aspect to the program, contact with interns from other disciplines, a mentor, a rotation through the agency.

Sometimes "intern" is just another way to spell "go-fer."

Since internships are usually offered to students, they usually only last for the summer.

From the agencies' perspective, internships can be a way of acquiring inexpensive assistance in return for the experience such an opportunity affords.

An internship can be a favor granted because someone you know has sufficient pull to get you in somewhere.

Or it can be a way for an agency to brand a promising junior so that person can be harvested after graduation.

In any case, internships are valuable, and I'd urge you to spend your summers in the employ of an advertising agency if you can.

You may be lucky enough to go to a school that actively promotes internships in the surrounding area.

If not, why not prepare a list of prospects and write them letters?

See what you can cook up.

Q. **If I can't afford to go to New York to knock on doors, is it okay to mail my mini-book?**

A. Yes, of course. But even better, if you have a Web site, include your URL on your résumé and in your e-mail and send that out instead. In a week or so, follow it up with a phone call or e-mail.

Calls from out-of-towners asking for appointments generally get a higher rate of response than local requests, so give it a try.

Make some appointments with creative recruiters, if you can.

Then, ask your folks to break out some frequent flyer miles for you. If you've got a buddy in New York who'll let you sleep on the sofa, your trip to New York may suddenly be more affordable than you thought.

Q. **If I've been looking for a while and it's not going so well, how do I know when to give up?**

A. If you're getting interviews, get feedback. As I've stated earlier, most people are loathe to be so honest that they cause some adorable stranger in front of them to cry.

If you suspect the worst, that your book is too average to compete, and you've done the best work you think you can do, you've got to ask for the famous "brutal" honesty.

Ask more than one person.

Tell them you really need to know the truth.

If you're given some encouragement, by all means continue. I have a theory about the learning-to-do-advertising process. I think it's like learning a new sport—like tennis or golf.

You're told that you are supposed to stand a certain way, put your weight on this or that foot, hold your wrist straight, or flexed, your head up or down. And you want to learn this sport and are trying hard to achieve what you can't really see or feel. One day you take a swing at a particular ball and everything you've learned falls into place automatically. The ball goes exactly where you want it, and beautifully. I think this is called muscle memory.

I've seen a similar thing happen with people who are learning advertising. Bad, boring ad follows bad, boring ad. The student, meanwhile, is working, analyzing, re-working, studying. Forming his or her own judgment. One day, seemingly effortlessly, this person creates his or her first killer ad.

It's a wonderful moment. To be clear, there's no substitute for talent. But some talent and lots of very hard work should pay off. Eventually.

So should you quit if you are advised to quit?

I believe you should weigh what you've been told, then decide for yourself whether to give up or to press on regardless.

Here's a true story.

A couple of years ago I met a young man at an ad club portfolio review. His name was Joey, he wanted to be an art director, and he wasn't having a good time.

"Please tell me what's wrong with my book," he said. "I know something's really wrong.

"I'm taking classes and working on my ads day and night, but it's been two years since I started looking, and I'm still unemployed. I used to think I was the victim of bad luck and bad timing, but now when I drop off my book, I get calls saying 'Thank you. Please pick up your book.' Then one of my friends from class gets the job. Lately, my classmates are telling me to go back to my old book. Like I'm getting worse."

I looked at Joey's book. He had some ideas in there, although not startling ones, and these frail things were buried beneath labored constructions of words and images so that it took a long time to get the messages Joey was trying to convey.

When I did "get" them, it was too late to feel anything except relief that I had figured it out.

And as for the art direction, no magic there either. Joey either had average talent or he had yet to develop an original graphic point of view. I asked Joey, reasonably, I thought, if he'd considered getting into some other line of work.

He said, "If I could think of something that turns me on as much as advertising, I would do it, because I feel so whipped. But I can't."

So, okay. I tried to help.

I noticed that Joey spoke colorfully when he was discussing his ad concepts. He was also a bit of a wise guy and words came out of his mouth in an interesting way. But somehow he seemed incapable of listening to himself and setting down his own words. He said he knew he would freeze up if he tape recorded himself, as I suggested he do.

I talked to Joey about getting back to basics—concentrating on products he knows and considering how a consumer might feel about those products, instead of striving for clever headlines that had tied him in knots and resulted in a collection of heartless executions.

Joey called me a day later. He wanted to talk to me about a hair gel he liked to use.

He said, "I have hair that's a different kind of problem every day." And I said, "I think you've got an idea there."

I wouldn't make up a happy ending just to close this story.

But it has a happy middle. Joey improved his book and got a job.

I saw his portfolio not long ago and I can only say that he was right to stick it out.

It's interesting how, upon occasion, a brave interviewer will say to an applicant, "You're really a nice person, but your book isn't too good. Why don't you go into another line of work?" At that point the would-be creative makes getting that creative job the focal point of his or her life. A commitment is made.

John tells this story about getting his first job.

John's first book had a lot of fun in it. People smiled a lot—in fact he generally had great interviews—but no job offers. One day he interviewed at an agency, and a creative supervisor told John his book was awful and why—out of twenty ads, only one had a glimmering of an idea.

John, to his credit, absorbed the blow and realized what had been going wrong for him.

He went back to school. At night. He really toiled over his book.

His work became very solid, and his sense of humor began working for the products he had chosen.

A year later, when he took this new book around, he had his pick of job offers. And the agency that gave him that "brutal" critique created a job for him.

There's a lot to be learned from John's story. If you keep hearing "good book, but no openings," and you don't get any substantive criticism, you may be getting the fast shuffle because nobody wants to level with you.

Which do you want? More pleasant interviews? Or the truth?

Take the truth. As with John, Joey, and countless others, you don't have to give up just because someone gives you a damning critique.

In fact, it may be just the push you need.

Another story.

A macho friend of mine admits that a particularly rough ad giant made him cry. Lee, who was an account executive at the time, dying to make the switch to creative, managed to hold back his tears until he was in the elevator. "He told me I should be selling shoes," Lee says.

Over a number of years, Lee had two more fairly devastating interviews with this man, and then, lo and behold, a job offer was made.

Lee turned the job down—not on principle, but because he had a better job by then—and now, a dozen years since that first traumatic interview, Lee is an executive creative director holding down one of those fancy salaries I was telling you about.

Yet another story.

Giff wanted to be a copywriter.

He was in fact, working in sales for a rivet company in New Jersey. He quit his job, took a $5,000 pay cut, and got his first copy job in a small agency.

Three weeks later, he was fired. The creative director told him to forget it. Said he was in the wrong business.

Giff didn't take no for an answer.

One week later, he had his second job at a top agency for more money. Today, Giff is a creative director and the winner of two Gold Lions from the Cannes Film Festival, among other awards, and he illustrated this book! Giff credits the creative director who fired him for getting him where he is today.

Last story.

An advertising superstar was invited to visit an advertising class at a university. He gave the class an assignment on one day and came back a couple of weeks later to review the work.

On that day, the ads were proudly tacked up on the wall. With his back to the class and his hands clasped behind his back, the superstar went from ad to ad, silently appraising for many long minutes each and every one.

Just as silently, the class awaited the critique of their efforts.

The moment came at last.

The superstar turned to face the assemblage. He spoke. "Everything on this wall is s—t," he said.

What happened?

My guess is adlike objects struck again.

Did the entire class drop their majors and transfer to biology?

Of course not. As a group, they and their professor used the critique as a learning experience. They worked even harder, and although I can't swear to it, I suspect that experience with that superstar was a turning point for a few.

So. As far as giving up is concerned, don't—not just because you can't find a job right away. Sometimes not finding a job has nothing to do with you.

Timing is important. Summer and the Christmas season can be bad times to look for work. Occasionally, the whole industry goes into a hiring slump.

I'd give your search a solid year if you are sure you're learning and your folks are willing to support your habit. Give it more time, up to two years, if you've found a job and are working on your book at night.

An interesting factoid: Most hires in the creative area interviewed at between thirty-five and seventy advertising agencies to get one offer. Seventy! That's one interview a week for almost a year and a half.

Does this depress you? Does this process seem too long, too tough, too uncertain?

Well, as my friend Renata says, "Pressure makes diamonds."

On the other hand, not everybody is meant to get into the creative side of advertising. If you've tried your best but the wall won't budge, there's no shame in saying "enough."

And just because ads aren't your thing, doesn't mean your creativity can't find another successful and satisfying outlet.

We all have to find what's right for us. Sometimes that means a few false starts on the road to a happy life.

Eric, a former copywriting aspirant I know, gave up his advertising agency job search after whatever he considered an appropriate amount of time. He opened a shoe store.

And not just any shoe store. It was a wonderful shoe store full of luscious Italian shoes. Two stores followed the first, for a chain of three, and Eric began designing his own brand of shoes, which were made up for him in Italy. Today, Eric is happy, rich, exercising his creative abilities, and I think it's safe to say that when he started his shoe business, he never looked back.

Maybe you're destined to have
a great career in advertising...but if not, there's
more than one way to succeed.

The hard truth is there are far fewer jobs at this level than the number of people who want them, so I guess that what's at work here is some Darwinian principal. Like natural selection.

The people with the best books, the people most suited to the rigors of the agency business will be hired, and the others will turn their talents to something else.

Q. **What if I'm really not cut out for advertising? Should I jump off the Brooklyn Bridge?**

A. What? And waste all that talent? Of course not!

Don't jump!

If you're a writer, start investigating public relations, journalism, publishing, sales promotion, retail. And don't consider these fields second best. They're all exciting, vital industries and may be the very best for you.

Look into other occupations altogether, and keep your writing alive by writing on your home time. Many novelists, playwrights, and poets have rent-paying work that gives them the financial support they need until their writing pays off.

If you're an art director, think about all the areas of graphic arts to be explored.

The burgeoning electronic universe is your playground. There are design studios and worlds of in-house graphics operations that involve many phases of packaging and promotion.

If you think your strength is illustration, check that out—maybe you can get started in retail, for instance, and work up a freelance business.

Or, for now, you can choose a field completely unrelated to art and exercise your artistic talents painting, drawing, and designing in your free time. Art for art's sake.

If you, like Joey from the story I told earlier, feel it's do advertising or die, keep in mind that your first job need not determine your life's work. You may want to get a job now and think about getting into advertising again next year.

Mark's first job was a package designer. Today he directs television commercials. In between these two careers Mark was an agency art director/producer and wrote commercials, too.

Gary's first job was in retail. His second was writing ads for a company that sold ad space on the inside of public toilet stalls.

Gary finally got that agency copy job and created a career for himself from copywriter all the way up to creative director on the West Coast.

He's now in Hollywood—a famous head-writer and producer of a fantastically successful TV show. He met the show's star when he was a copywriter and the star did commercials for his account.

Q. **I'm a senior, about to graduate. Our final critique is coming up soon. Could you go over the most common portfolio mistakes one more time? How about a list?**

A. My pleasure.

The Ten Most Commonly Made Portfolio Mistakes

1. Heartless ads. Slick headlines, puns for the sake of making wordplays, ads that seem to be ads but there's nothing inside.

Heartless ads are the result of using the computer to make adlike objects before you've come up with an original concept. You didn't spend enough time getting to know your product and your consumer. Instead, you jumped to a seemingly clever execution.

2. Walking strategy statements. These are also called adlike objects. They have their roots in research, their creators understand their product and the marketplace, but the resulting work has no zing.

Heartless ads, walking strategy statements, and boring, unoriginal un-advertising turns interviewers into gibbering, inarticulate fools. They want to help you, but they can't figure out where to start. We want to see original ideas that make us feel something.

3. The casual use of celebrity spokespersons. We want to see selling ideas, and grafting a celebrity artist or pitchman onto your campaign is not an idea. It's an execution, and generally, an easy way out.

4. Too much clutter. Storyboards and radio scripts that your reviewers may not take time to read. Filler ads to round out a campaign. Filler campaigns to fluff up a book. Miscellaneous freelance projects that simply take up space.

When in doubt, take it out.

5. Too much public service advertising. One or two poignant ads to spotlight a worthy cause is fine, but more than a few and we know you're taking the easy course.

6. A sloppy-looking presentation. Make your book look professional. Sure roughs are okay, but not with food stains.

It's okay to put in last night's brilliant idea before you've had a chance to work it up. Otherwise, make your book look as good as you do. Same goes for you Web site.

7. Crude, rude, sexist, racist, or vulgar advertising. Bad taste is bad news.

8. Too many ads. You can't edit your work, and that's too bad.

If you can't tell your good ads from your bad ones, you've got a long way to go.

But everyone tells you something different, you say.

You're confused. Of course you are. Listen to the critics, stand back, and make some judgment calls yourself.

Some confusion is understandable, but you'll feel dumb standing up for ads you don't like if you're only keeping them in your book because someone else liked them.

Start editing your own work, now.

Take out your worst campaigns.

It's okay if your book is a little thin.

Replace your worst ads with killers as you get better.

9. "Faddy" topics and a book full of class assignments. This says you haven't taken the job of getting a job seriously.

10. No résumé. So who are you, anyway? And how are we supposed to call you and offer you a job if we don't have your phone number? We know you're in a state of panic right now, but take ten minutes and bang out something simple on your Mac.

This could be the most worthwhile ten minutes you ever spent.

We knew you could do it all along.

What's next? Something a little special.

The next section is titled "A Little Help from Some Friends."

You'll meet creative directors, executive creative directors, CEOs, and people who just got started.

In this section, you'll hear a few things you've heard before—that it's essential to start with the product and the consumer, and that your ads must make people feel something.

But you'll also hear a few things you never heard before.

Like why you should think horizontal, not vertical. Why you should kill all your darlings. Why your salary is not an indication of your personal worth. Or how to make $500,000 a year before you're thirty.

And lots more. Each and every one of the following essays is a rare treat, so get ready to enjoy yourself.

Now you know everything I can tell you. I loved writing this book and hope that it's helpful. If it is, we'd like to hear from you. We'll be updating this book again in the future and your tales from the job market might be part of it. Just as those before you have contributed to this book, your comments could help those who come after you.

Send an e-mail to me at npb@wwnorton.com when you get your first job in advertising.

I've got my fingers crossed for you.

PART III

A LITTLE HELP FROM SOME FRIENDS

(Advice on how to make it from some people who made it.)

SUM OF ALL PARTS

BY DAVID BALDWIN

Executive Producer of the film *Art & Copy* and Founder & Chief Creative Officer of Baldwin&

A good start to an integrated campaign is figuring out what integration means. Over the last decade, we've seen many buzzwords come and go. "New paradigm," anyone? Or how about "proactive synergy to create empowerment for the dynamic framework of the entire enterprise engaging the Log Tail utilizing Web 2.0"?

Somewhere, I guarantee it, that sentence is in an agency's new business credentials.

As I look around, one of the longest-lasting, most tenacious buzzwords has to be the word *integration*. (Actually, now that I think of it, *buzzword* is a buzzword, isn't it? But I digress.)

Every award show has a category for it. And when a buzzword gets its own category, you know it's here to stay for a while.

The issue is that when agencies talk about integration and when clients talk about integration, they often mean something completely different.

When clients talk about it, they're referring to the way the entire enchilada works. How the product flows from inception to manufacturing the messaging. How the people in the company work and speak. How the call center interacts with customers and the company. And how everything should be moving in the right direction.

When I hear agencies talk about integration, they're often talking about an integrated idea. How a brand idea, and sometimes just a smaller brand effort, works together with many moving pieces. The biggest mistake I hear agencies make is when they talk about integration as simply having the interactive be a big part of the communication plan. It happens all the time and it's kind of laughable.

There's a difference between integration and an integrated campaign.

Of course, the work that has been entered and won in the integrated categories of the One Show and others have been fantastic, but that's not what we're talking about.

If you want to see integration from the client's point of view, look no further than Hannah Montana on Disney's Web site. You're probably already very familiar with Hannah if you have a daughter who's eight to thirteen years old.

A warning: If you haven't already experienced her, you'll have to subject yourself to the Disney/Industrial complex. But if you can stand it you'll see what I mean. A note to diabetics—

all of the sweetener here, though plentiful, is artificial.

You have characters, music, videos, a television show, games, CDs, downloads, a concert series, songwriters churning out on-brand work, CRM to keep the kiddies involved, and much more. All from brand to manufacturing to digital and physical output. It's pretty much a marvel in integration.

Now, there's a schedule to make for all of this, so the songs have to be written and recorded, producers hired, CDs manufactured and delivered, shows written and filmed, and the campaign launched, all by a specific date.

You'll notice that advertising is only a small part of the effort.

This is what clients mean by integration. And when agencies come in and talk about their integrated offering, clients often shake their heads.

Now imagine if agencies came from a place this big and applied the craft of our business to the process. They wouldn't be able to do it all, but they would be unstoppable.

There are some companies getting close, but mostly agencies are still concerned with churning out television spots and wondering where their business is going.

The business hasn't left—it's just changed and there's a huge possibility here to train our creativity square at this new world because believe me, it not only needs our talent, it's going there with or without us.

ONE OF THE MOST AWARDED COPYWRITERS AND CREATIVE DIRECTORS IN THE BUSINESS TODAY, DAVID BALDWIN IS THE FOUNDER OF THE NEWLY FORMED BALDWIN&. FOR THE PREVIOUS FIVE YEARS, DAVID WAS THE CHAIRMAN OF THE ONE CLUB IN NYC, THE FORCE BEHIND THE ONE SHOW. ALONGSIDE HIS CREATIVE ADVERTISING EXPLOITS, DAVID IS AN EXECUTIVE PRODUCER FOR THE FILM *ART & COPY*, AND A GUITARIST/ SONGWRITER FOR THE BAND *PANTS*, WHOSE CD, *TWICE THE SNAKE YOU NEED*, CAN BE FOUND ON ITUNES OR AMAZON.COM. THIS ESSAY FIRST APPEARED IN *ONE: A MAGAZINE*; REPRINTED FROM *ONE: A MAGAZINE*, WITH PERMISSION OF YASH EGAMI; COPYRIGHT OF THE ONE CLUB.

HOW DO YOU SUCCEED IN A BUSINESS THAT HASN'T BEEN REINVENTED YET?

BY TOM CUNNIFF

VP, Associate Creative Director/Director of Interactive Communications, Combe Incorporated

You are hurtling at 900 mph toward a career in advertising.

The awards book your eyes are glued to is the rearview mirror.

Oh, and here's the brick wall you're about to slam into: nobody knows what a "career in advertising" is going to mean anymore because it's all being re-invented.

This is either the craziest time in the past eighty years to take a creative job in advertising, or the absolute best. Now more than ever, advertising needs muscular, adventurous, wild minds. The very best minds—maybe yours—will not just create commercials, or digital widgets or viral videos, but will help invent what advertising can be.

OK, so now you know advertising is going to be a sort of glorious mess. How do you succeed in a business that hasn't been reinvented yet? I suggest five things.

1. Think horizontal, not vertical. You'll have to be great at creating ads if you want to get a job and keep it. But, that's not enough. Get outside your comfort zone. Learn, learn, learn. Make friends with different kinds of people, and ask them to teach you: marketing MBAs, PR people, computer geeks, Web analytics gurus, market researchers, lawyers, accountants, etc. Talk to your clients and learn their business. Don't buy into the "us vs. them" nonsense, or the absurd fallacy that clients are idiots. These are sucker's games invented by insecure creatives. Develop a network of people who know things you don't and nurture that network as if your career depends on it. Because in fact, it does.

2. Learn by doing. Screw theory. Dive in, experiment. Start a blog. Get on Twitter. Put some pictures up on Flickr. Always, always, always look to the horizon and try to understand what's coming next. Try different stuff. When you get lucky, try to understand why. And don't be an arrogant knucklehead when you do get lucky. The universe has a ton of humble pie that it's just waiting to feed to creative people whose egos get too big. And yes, in my past I have been forced to eat my share.

3. Think globally. Madison Avenue is not the center of the ad universe anymore. Neither is America. There are billions of people out there just as creative as you are, and advertising can be outsourced just like everything else. Advertising follows opportunity, and during your career that's likely to happen in Asia. Pay close attention to what the CEOs of WPP, Publicis, and Omnicom are saying and keep an open mind about it. Read as much as you can about other cultures, especially China and India. Learn the language and go visit if you can. In your career, imagination won't be enough. You need to constantly demonstrate that you are someone who makes problems shrink and possibilities grow. Speaking of which...

4. Always focus on possibility. Change will be constant, and many changes will be hugely disruptive. Some, deeply painful. Whatever happens, always ask yourself: "what new possibilities does this create?" Remember the most wrenching change you encounter may also lead to the best part of your advertising career. Stay open.

5. Talk to strangers. Get in the habit of saying hello to people you don't know, especially if they seem to offer challenging ideas. In fact if you think I've said anything useful here, you can start by saying hello to me. Follow me on Twitter (@tjcnyc) or look me up on social networking sites like LinkedIn. The only ground rules: cover letters, résumés, and self-promotion will earn you a place in my spam filter. Intelligent questions and insights will earn you respect and prompt replies.

Advertising is undergoing radical change, so it favors people with guts now more than ever before. Don't be afraid to be creative.

As the famous jazz pianist Thelonious Monk once said..."The only cats worth anything are the cats who take chances. Sometimes, I play things I never heard myself."

TOM CUNNIFF IS A HYBRID TRADITIONAL/INTERACTIVE CREATIVE EXECUTIVE WHO HAS WORKED FOR BRANDS AT AT&T, UNILEVER, HEWLETT-PACKARD, AND COMBE. HIS CAREER HAS GIVEN HIM AN UNUSUAL 360-DEGREE PERSPECTIVE. HE'S WORKED AT BIG AD AGENCIES, STARTED A SMALL INTERACTIVE AGENCY THAT WAS LATER ACQUIRED BY AN E-COMMERCE AGENCY, AND TODAY TOM WORKS ON THE CLIENT SIDE AT COMBE INCORPORATED IN WHITE PLAINS, NY.

CONTROLLING PAIN

BY GREG DiNOTO

CEO/Creative Director, DiNoto Inc.

I remember putting my book together and getting my first job in advertising. It was like being beaten by a cat-o'-nine-tails made from piano wire and porcelain clown figurines. In the interest of offsetting the sensations you are about to experience, I humbly offer some various thoughts and items and such that might be of use.

1. Be an animal. This business rewards the hungry and relentless.

2. Conceive with the heart, defend with the head. The creatives I hire are two-channel people. The first channel is about talent. The second channel is about maturity. It's the ability to become coldly rational when it's time to assess your own work and ultimately defend it. This ability to separate yourself emotionally from your work leads to better work. It gives you credibility with your partner, your creative director, and your clients. And it means a better chance of keeping great work intact despite the incessant onslaught of opinion that goes with the business. Be passionately dispassionate. Mr. Spock never lost an argument.

3. Bitch later. Whether it's putting your book together, getting an appointment with that great agency, or struggling to keep a great campaign alive, put your head down and make things happen before you indulge in an orgy of complaint. The reason is simple. Complaining is a mindset. The more you hear yourself do it, the easier it becomes to blame external forces when things don't go your way. You become your excuses. You forgive yourself. You compromise. You lose. You die. So don't talk about putting the book together. Put the book together. It's the hardest assignment you'll ever have. But when it's done you'll have reason to celebrate instead of bitch.

4. Don't be a writer or an art director. Those terms tend to stultify your thinking. Great advertising is not about coming up with headlines and visuals. It's about coming up with campaign ideas. So approach your assignment by thinking about a unique interplay of visual and verbal components. The *relationship* between words and visuals should make me understand the point of the campaign in an ownable way. So think of yourself as a conceptual engineer or an idea architect. It will make you a better writer or art director.

5. Don't populate the landing page for your site with a Flash movie of orangutans making love. Don't cover your portfolio in pink fur. Or sequins. Or staves of baleen. It makes you seem breathless and desperate for attention. Your portfolio isn't an arts-and-crafts project. It's the best evidence that you can intuit and argue and persuade with great campaign ideas. Like many things in life, it's what's inside that counts. Don't decorate. Fortify.

6. **Feed your head.** Go to a bullfight. Sing at Wigstock. Subscribe to the ballet. Copulate. Read. It will keep you stimulated now and sane later.

7. Don't do campaigns for the following: Hot sauce. Topless bars. Lingerie. Homeless shelters. Or anything with the word "extreme" in it. These subjects are easy. They have built-in excitement or emotional equity. And they're done to death—especially in junior books.

8. Don't present what you're not proud of. I'd rather see a book with three great campaigns than one with three great campaigns and two mediocre ones. It says you're discriminating. That you can edit yourself. And it should remain law once you land a job. Never present a campaign that you don't want to produce—it will be the one that gets produced.

9. Don't be a backslapper or an a–kisser. Stay focused on the work. It's what makes money for your boss.

10. All important work is great work, but not all great work is important work. Important work moves the business forward. It becomes part of the culture. It's new. It's challenging. Maybe a little frightening. Strive for important work.

PRIOR TO STARTING HIS OWN AGENCY IN 1997, GREG DiNOTO WAS EXECUTIVE CREATIVE DIRECTOR AT DEUTSCH ADVERTISING, WHERE HE SPEARHEADED AWARD-WINNING CAMPAIGNS ON ACCOUNTS INCLUDING TANQUERAY GIN, PROMOFLOR, AND IKEA. HE'S BEEN RECOGNIZED WITH NUMEROUS INDUSTRY AWARDS AND HAS BEEN NAMED TO *ADWEEK'S* CREATIVE ALL-STAR LIST.

THE RIGHT WORD

BY JIM DURFEE

Former Partner & Copywriter, Messner Vetere Berger McNamee Schmetterer Euro RSCG, New York

"The difference between the right word and the almost right word is the difference between lightning and a lightning bug."

Mark Twain said that. And if you don't have a comparable reverence for aptness I suggest you forget about being a copywriter right now. Account work would be nice.

Mark Twain also said, "Kill your darlings." In other words, beware of those cutesy phrases that are written to show off one's cleverness.

And don't try to be funny. Above all, don't try to be funny. Try to be interesting. If it turns out to be funny, great. You'll have humor without strain. The only kind that really works.

(So you think being a copywriter is fun, or something?)

Here's something to think about.

The difference between a weak headline and a strong headline is more a matter of perseverance than talent. Like the miner panning for gold—keep sifting the sand until at last (!), there's a bright shining nugget worth its weight in sales.

Another way you'll know you have a strong headline is when you've written one that doesn't require a subhead to support it. Never use subheads except to break up long body copy.

Never write to masses, because advertising does not appear before the masses. Not on TV. Only one or two (or three or four) people see a TV commercial at a time. And only one person reads a magazine at a time. So write to that one person.

Get a picture in your mind of who he/she is and write to that person only. You'll be surprised at how much more intelligent you'll sound, and how much more effective you'll be.

There's a tiresome, endless argument that people don't read long copy. Nonsense. People will read what interests them. No matter how long it is. Which means there's only "too long" copy. And that can be a mere few words if they aren't the right words.

Here's another piece of advertising nonsense that won't die: "Don't write **negative** headlines, because people react better to positive things." Would you call the following statement negative or positive: "Don't step back or you'll fall off the cliff."

When you have your copy honed to the point where you think it's ready, suck in your breath and cut it by 20–30 percent and you'll have stronger copy.

Use little words rather than big words. Say it as simply and directly as possible. Trust your gut as much as your head.

And above all, never forget that an ad can never be good enough.

Uh…good luck.

"THE FAULKNER OF BODY COPY," JIM DURFEE HAS TRAINED AND NURTURED SOME OF THE TOP TALENTS IN THE BUSINESS. HE WAS A COFOUNDER OF CARL ALLY INC. AND A PARTNER IN DURFEE SOLO ADVERTISING. VOTED ONE OF THE TEN BEST COPYWRITERS IN AMERICA BY *ADDAY*, FEATURED IN *HOW THE WORLD'S BEST ADVERTISING WRITERS WRITE THEIR ADS*, MR. DURFEE WAS INDUCTED INTO THE ONE CLUB CREATIVE HALL OF FAME IN 1997.

fig. a: lightning

fig. b: lightning bug

THE ART OF SALARY NEGOTIATION

BY DOREEN DVORIN

Writer/Thinker at Kamikaze Creative

1. Salary has nothing to do with personal worth.

2. Salary has nothing to do with what you think you need/deserve.

3. It's just money. No magic elixir, statement of value, bluebird of happiness. An exchange: I give you great ads; you give me your name on my résumé. Learn to separate cash from emotions. You'll earn more.

4. One way or another, everyone lies about money. You know it. They know it.

5. The cliché is Win-Win Negotiation—having fun reaching an agreement everyone feels good about.

6. Life is negotiation. Which movie you and your friends see, how much you spend on vacation versus how much you pay Visa, what you earn. You've been doing it for decades.

7. Can't reconcile salary? Accounts, creative groups, expenses, health-insurance upgrades. Continuing education, offices, personal days, start dates, moving expenses, paid honeymoons, reviews, raises, bonuses versus wages (always take salary), yadda, yadda. All are fair and negotiable currency. Don't ask. Assume they are yours. (It's not "Do you pay moving expenses?" It's "Do you have a contract mover, or do you want me to get a few estimates?")

8. What someone else offers has nothing to do with the current negotiation.

9. What you earn now is irrelevant to the income you're negotiating. Every position/agency/week/month/year/account goal/situation is different. Don't reveal what you make or what your goal is.

10. Every position has a salary range. Some salaries are tied to titles. Some to candidate desirability/availability. Others are strictly budgetary. Ranges may—or may not—be final.

11. It is your duty to find out what the spread is—low to high. You want The Most. If you listen, someone might tell you what that is. School placement offices can help. Headhunters may. Friends in that market—same agency or not. If you're not shy, ask your interviewers. Their answers will usually be in the low-mid range. Build up the job. Build up how much they want you. They'll build up the money.

12. The agency's goal is profitability. Most agencies (especially big shops) must fit you into their salary/title/position mold. Most are not trying to cheat you. They may be handicapped by corporate policies but they want Win-Win endings, too.

13. Don't blurt out numbers. Let them. No matter what they say, don't laugh. Ask for details. Annual bonuses? Salary reviews? Percentages? Big agencies don't always pay less. Or more. Neither do smaller shops. Uncover the range. Go for it.

14. Name a figure and you could sell yourself short. Worse, you could offend them with Inflated Income Arrogance. Whatever you say, you're stuck with it. When they ask, ask back. Let them build up the job's importance/responsibilities. Be humble. Agreeable. When it comes back to dollars, say "That's a big job, isn't it? How much did you say it pays?" If they say they didn't, ask now. No matter how much they offer, ask if there's flexibility (never "Is that all?") No? Start negotiating other stuff. Even if their offer is more than you thought you'd ever get.

15. "Circus/Miami Ad/UT grads get $_____ to start" is not The Correct Answer. Try the *I'm-just-a-junior-you're-so-much-more-experienced-what-did-you-say-the-job-pays?* routine.

16. You're surrounded by a hundred other portfolios. So what? They're negotiating with you. Don't let competition intimidate you. Don't let the fact that they want you inflate your hat size. A negotiation is not an offer. Yet.

17. If you use a Better Offer to up the ante, be prepared to take it. If you use a Pretend Offer, be prepared to stay unemployed.

18. Employers don't want employees to discuss salary. The range is easier to hide if they don't. People erroneously equate wages with Personal Worth. Egos inflate. Emotions rage. Many factors influence income (market timing, experience, negotiating skills, etc.) No one else's deal has anything to do with yours. You just want the range.

19. Big shops with well-defined training programs may have One Deal. Vacations, accounts, offices, etc. may be negotiable. Salary is not. What's more important—working for that agency or making more money?

20. When they make an offer, you don't have to say Yes! immediately. If you have scheduled other interviews, tell them. Make it a benefit. You're thrilled, psyched, ready to go—but an appointment is a commitment. You want to start with no doubts, no guilt—just pure, unwavering enthusiasm. They want someone serious about making—and keeping—commitments. Don't they?

21. Never forget that it's not your soul you're negotiating—just money.

22. There are fewer jobs in a down market. Not fewer *new* jobs. Award-show All Stars and low-end-of-the-salary-totem Juniors all collect unemployment.

23. Just because the job market stinks, good shops don't always cut what they'll pay a hot prospect. Providing it's someone they really, really want.

24. One way or another, you *earned* that salary negotiation. By bagging a student One Show Pencil or something chic from Cannes. By making CMYK and putting together an amazing book. By possessing the talent, cool factor, confidence, and competitiveness any job market requires.

25. Creative directors you want to work for are always trolling for talent. Top students at top schools still get multiple offers—some before they graduate.

26. If they're negotiating, Uncle/Aunt CD wants YOU. Not just another good Junior.

27. CDs and recruiters know the true value of Top Talent and still want it, no matter what the economy's doing. (If you're less than Top, well—there's always being in the right place at the right time. Keep working on your book, pick up experience any way you can, build your network, stay in touch with every CD/ACD/AD or CW you talk to—no recession lasts forever).

28. Even exceptional shops with growing client lists have a very short list of desirable choices. Don't panic over school debt just because the job market stinks. Original Point #16—in fact, Points #1–21—still hold.

29. Reread #s 13–14 as many times as it takes to own them. Hold your tongue. Make them reveal the range.

30. No matter how low the offer, don't be insulted. Do not blink, smirk, swallow hard, or laugh out loud.

31. If the range is Way Too Low, they're not used to hiring top Juniors and have no idea of going rates. Or it's a sweat shop taking advantage of the economy to make a creative killing.

32. There are good, honest shops with CDs you want to work for who don't panic in a down market. If one of them makes a low offer, maybe they're in a less expensive city. They may be in an "expansion bubble," needing help, not being quite ready to afford it, but still willing to risk the right new hire. If it'll pay the rent and your student loans, if you can build your book and get good experience, talk the money up as high as you can, then practice Point #7: Everything—and anything—is still negotiable.

33. If you're already working in the industry—interning, freelance, in an agency/client/media category you don't want to label you forever, let them know its The Work, not money, that's important. You can live on what you're earning now, even if you can't afford imported beer. After they make their first offer, remind them. It's The Work. And Gosh, I have *that* much. To move to (*insert expensive city here*) it'd take this much to equal what I make now. The real work I've gotten makes me an experienced Junior who'll be productive from Day One. Now, how much did you say the job pays?

34. If you have another good offer, reread #8 and #17 before you bargain with it.

35. Look them in the eye. Look eager. Sincere. Then Shut Up. In a down market too many candidates think they have to settle for 20% less than they are/were/expect to be making. In fact, agencies will ante up to 10% more for the right candidate. That's the caveat—and it's a biggie. *For the right candidate.*

36. If the offer's still low and you really want the job, revisit Point #7: there are things you can negotiate up besides salary. Be smart, creative. Try reviews/raises/bonuses based not just on length of employment—but on awards won, new accounts landed, completing a learning curve and/or stepping up to more responsibility.

37. A generous, award-winning, visible mentor is one of best career perks you can negotiate. As are award-enabling clients. I'm not saying pawn the dog and take an unlivable financial hit—I'm saying include them *plus* all the money and cool stuff you can get. (All offers being more or less equal, that's what'd get me in any kind of market—not another $2,000-$5,000 and a window office.) If the agency has people like that, negotiate yourself into their immediate orbit.

38. Never take a job strictly for the money; 99.9% of the time that salary will be moot—you'll be so desperate, you'll take anything from anyone, just to get out of there.

39. Whatever you negotiate, get it in writing. Ask for a confirmation letter captioning your entire package—in detail. Salary, perks, accounts, team members, vacations, offices, moving expenses, per diems, reviews, start date—leave nothing out. Many shops do it automatically, but still ask. Read it, make sure it's correct. Fix any errors/omissions. When it's done, show up on time.

40. The key to negotiating Up in a Down market? Knowing where you fit into the grand scheme of available Juniors. Knowing where the hiring agency fits into the grand scheme of shops you want to work for. Knowing the going rate, regardless which (Up or Down) market you're in. Knowing what else you want (besides more money) or can settle for before you book the interview.

If you get in a bind, let me know. I'll do my best to help you keep your mouth shut and that cool, confident face forward.

DOREEN DVORIN ESTABLISHED THE FIRST PORTFOLIO SCHOOL COPYWRITING DEPARTMENT AND HAS TAUGHT AT PORTFOLIO CENTER, CREATIVE CIRCUS, EMORY UNIVERSITY, AND OTHER FINE INSTITUTIONS. SHE'S STILL TEACHING—DOING AGENCY, ASSOCIATION, AND CORPORATE WORKSHOPS ON CREATIVE STRATEGY, COPYWRITING, PRESENTATION, SALARY NEGOTIATION, AND A DOZEN OTHER SUBJECTS. STILL FREELANCING. STILL EDITING HER BOOK(S). CAN STILL BE REACHED AT KAMIKAZECREATIVE@GMAIL.COM. THIS ESSAY FIRST APPEARED IN *CMYK MAGAZINE*, © 2002; REPRINTED WITH PERMISSION OF CURTIS CLARKSON.

HOW TO GET HEADHUNTERS TO DO BACK FLIPS FOR YOU

BY HEIDI EHLERS

Founder of Black Bag creative recruitment + career management inc.

Distinguish yourself as being one of the best that every headhunter wants to know.

1. Learn what we headhunters do and who we do it for.

Sorry to break it to you but, headhunters do not work for you, the talent. They work for the company that is seeking talent. Some might tell you they work for the talent, and will promise to send your work to as many agencies as possible, whether or not there is an opening. However, many creative directors have told me that it's annoying to have recruiters send them unsolicited work, especially since you've already sent that same creative director your work yourself. When headhunters send unsolicited work to creative directors it could lead to a dispute over whether the headhunter should get paid for that unsolicited introduction, and, well, that potential expense could cost you getting hired.

So, remember, headhunters work for the company. They are hired by the company. The company hires them because they realize that headhunters talk to WAY more people than they do; this is what headhunters do ten hours a day, and this is what headhunters specialize in: getting to know the market; getting to know who the best people are out there. And, if you're one of the best people, getting to know you.

2. Be patient.

It addition to getting to know the market, headhunters need to stay focused and find the best people to fill the jobs they've been contracted by agencies to fill. So you may call a headhunter and they may have something for you right away, or they may not. But be patient. They will want to take the time to get to know you and find out if you're one of the best.

3. Don't call a headhunter just because you're having a sh*t day.

Call a headhunter only when you're ready—ready to make the next step in your career, ready with a book that is prepared and professionally pulled together. Both an old-school copy and an online copy. Ready can also mean, "I've been thinking of these two routes. Route A makes sense because of this. Route B makes sense because of this. My goal is this, so which route do you think will get me closer to my goal?" But do some of the thinking in advance of the call. Don't reflex. Don't react. Go for a walk around the block instead.

4. Tell us everything.

You called us, didn't you? You must want to talk about something that is happening in your career. So, don't get all "Oh I don't want to talk about it" when we meet with you. Tell us why you wanted to meet with us, and what you're hoping we will do for you. Tell us what the perfect job looks like for you. Now, in one year, and in five years. Ten would put us over the top.

Tell us who else you're meeting, why what you're considering interests you, and what your concerns are.

Tell us your dreams, tell us your goals, tell us why those goals and dreams are important to you. Tell us who or what inspires you. Tell us what work you wish you'd done. Tell us what you've read recently that taught you something new. Tell us what you see happening in the world of communications. Where is it going? What is happening that is different from what was happening five years ago?

Agencies want to hire people who are turned on and super-charged and excited by the world around them. Agencies want to hire creative people who understand accountability and results. Agencies want to hire creative people who understand that their clients care about results. So if we ask you, after you've said that the campaign did really well, what the spike in sales was, know the answer.

5. Interview back.

See if the recruiter who is interviewing you knows his stuff. Does he have a thought or two, study creativity on a global level, read, maintain an expertise in the business and what's happening where? I don't mean gossip. Gossip is transitory and has a shelf life of maybe 24 hours. Who cares. I mean the stuff that really matters: leadership, presentation skills, courage, decision making, presence, strategic thought, networking—oh, and an understanding of how to make money and keep making money in this business.

6. Brand yourself.

Be proud. Stick out your chest. Show off what makes you uniquely you. Tell us your story. Tell us what makes you different. Tell us what makes you a great hire. Tell us what you stink at, and what you're doing about it, and by when. Come with a brand plan. Do some thinking about who you are and what you want. Think of your plan, and tell us what it is. Put us to task. Ask questions. Solicit feedback. Demand brutal honesty. Make us tell you what you need to do to be considered one of the best—the best that we'll proudly and fiercely endorse to our clients, the clients that are dying to hire the best talent they possibly can.

7. Make us tell you what is wrong with the job.

There are no perfect jobs. There are no perfect people. Because you've given us such a great understanding of who you are, we now know what you might not like about this particular job. And what obstacles you might encounter. So you can make the appropriate decisions, and not go into this job blind. Ask. Arm yourself. Demand honesty back in exchange for the honesty you've given us. Develop a relationship.

8. Don't let your friends run your career.

Would you go to an accountant, get her professional opinion, then have your aunt review and revise your income tax return? Would you visit a lawyer then do what your best friend says to do instead? Recruiters—oh sorry, headhunters—see a lot of people do a lot of things with their careers, some good, some bad, some confusing, some inspiring. They also see a lot of portfolios and know which ones stand out, and why they do. They are willing to, and in fact want to, share with you what they've learned, and can't figure out why your friend Cindy's opinion matters more than an expert's.

9. Help us find you.

This one point alone will make you stand out from everyone else and make us love you. It's funny, in other industries, people seem to get that. Tell the headhunter where to find you so he can regularly call you with jobs. You can say no, you can pass, but it's important to know about the stuff that's out there.

Headhunters are messengers of opportunity. Make it easy for opportunity to find you. Send us an e-mail, tell us where you are.

10. Take charge of your career.

Be in charge of your career, your life, your future. Do you know what my dream interview is? I have had one like this in eleven years. Here's what happened: He showed up with an amazing book. It was impeccably presented. He took me through each piece in his book and told me why he created it, what it was for, why he chose to do what he did, the results his work created for his client, and what awards it won. (Every piece had won an award.) He told me how much money he made, how much money he wanted to make, what he was good at, what work he loved, what kinds of jobs I should call him about, why he thought he was qualified for those jobs, what he was learning, what his goal was, when he was going to achieve that goal, his plan to achieve that goal. During the entire meeting, he was pleasant, engaging, listened well, had interesting points of view, shared some personal stories, was honest, and open, and collaborative.

Guess what?

Today he is one of North America's most sought-after creative directors. No surprise. I did back flips for him then. I'd do back flips for him today. Any recruiter would.

HEIDI EHLERS IS FOUNDER OF BLACK BAG CREATIVE RECRUITMENT + CAREER MANAGEMENT INC. FOR FIFTEEN YEARS, SHE HAS SPECIALIZED IN THE HIRING OF CREATIVE TALENT—THOSE ELUSIVE SOULS THAT ARE THE CATALYSTS FOR ANY COMPANY. SHE CREATED DIARY OF A CREATIVE DIRECTOR BECAUSE SHE WANTED TO KNOW: DO CREATIVE PEOPLE WHO ACHIEVE UBER-SUCCESS THINK AND BEHAVE DIFFERENTLY? THE LEARNING FROM DIARY OF A CREATIVE DIRECTOR CREATED CAMP BLACK BAG, A PROGRAM THAT TEACHES CREATIVES HOW TO STRATEGIZE A GREAT CAREER. SHE FOUNDED THE TALENT ATTRACTION INSTITUTE—A METHODOLOGY TO HELP COMPANIES FILL THEIR TALENT PIPE WITH THE WORLD'S BEST CREATIVE TALENT. BLACK BAG TALENT ATTRACTION AND ACQUISITION IS THE MOTHERSHIP: A TALENT CONSULTANCY SPECIALIZING IN CREATIVE TALENT, CREATIVE DEPARTMENTS, AND CREATIVE CAREERS. THIS ARTICLE FIRST APPEARED ON BLACKBAGONLINE.COM; REPRINTED WITH PERMISSION.

SHOPPING FOR ADS

BY JEFFREY EPSTEIN

Director of Chicago Portfolio School

I have a copywriter friend whom I met when she attended Chicago Portfolio. But before she spent one day making ads, she already had an incredibly intuitive sense of how to make an ad great. That's because she is, and has always been, a major-league shopper.

I'm not talking about a *Consumer Reports* shopper—someone dedicated to all the gory details about specs, prices, ratings, etc. I'm talking a power shopper, in which tough marketing and sales decisions are made quickly based on feel and instinct.

Want proof? OK. She owns nine pairs of Diesel jeans.

Remarkable as that might seem, that's not what impresses me.

What's truly wonderful is that she can tell you why she owns nine pairs of Diesel jeans. Better yet, why she needs nine pairs of Diesel jeans.

Just ask and she'll tell you all about the wash, the fit, the style, the color, the cut, the best place to buy them (new and used)—maybe even the history of the brand. And the advertising, of course.

But it's not just jeans. She also happens to be an extraordinarily good shopper of lots of other things, like watches, cheese, sushi, cars, and sneakers. At first I wasn't sure what to make of her ninja shopping skills, but then it occurred to me: the qualities that make a great shopper are the exact same qualities that make a great advertising creative.

She becomes an expert on the product, but also the category. She knows the competition inside and out. She understands the target market (young jeans-buying women) and has an innate sense of what feels right and wrong about the advertising and marketing. Malcolm Gladwell (and my grandmother) call this being a *Maven*.

And even though my friend has never taken the factory tour or sat through a client briefing, she develops an innate sense of what feels right and wrong about the advertising and marketing.

Most importantly, she genuinely respects the products she buys.

Which is exactly the kind of resolute thinking you should engage in when making ads, especially when you're doing spec ads for your book, where there's no mandated brand, let alone direction or strategy.

Dan Wieden is a copywriter and founder of Wieden & Kennedy, a tiny agency in Portland, Oregon, that became a big, hugely successful agency based on their ability to make ads that connect similarly with customers for their longtime client NIKE. But they didn't do it that way right out of the box. First, they had to learn the lesson of thinking like a shopper too, according to Dan: "What we thought were great pieces of advertising were rejected out of hand as being phony. And what we learned slowly over time is to quit talking to other ad people. And not write our ads for award show judges. But to write to tennis players or basketball players or runners."

By the way, in the big agency world, there's a word for thinking like a customer. It's called *planning*, and it's a helpful market-research discipline that has assisted in many great ad campaigns. But regardless of what you call it, caring a lot about the product ultimately will lead to a purchase.

Here's what doesn't work when you sit down to make an ad:

- **Knowing nothing meaningful about the category or product you're advertising**
- **Having no insight into what people want from the category or product**
- **Distancing yourself from the product or the buying experience because you don't like the product or you've never bought one.**

When you have no insight, your ads are irrelevant. When you have no passion for the product, your ads are dull. And when you distance yourself, your ads are the kind of smug and self-serving, tongue-in-cheek work seen all too often in ad-school student books.

Ads like that remind me of mother-in-law jokes, and they're about as tired. Sure, it's an easy laugh, but so what? When the humor of the ad is simply a put-down of the product, the category, or the customers, you've produced nothing but a smug nod and wink to the other, as Dan Wieden points out, advertising smart-asses.

By the way, I hope the people who make ads never start thinking they are cooler than the people who buy the products. Just because you only eat organic, whole-wheat, bread does not make it OK to make fun of Wonder Bread.

Presumably, people who buy Wonder Bread (and according to the latest official statistics, the approximate number of Wonder Bread consumers is three trillion) do so because they like it.

Don't actually buy the product you're advertising? Pretend you do. Don't like it? Who cares? Learn to like it. A lot. Like it, love it, enjoy it, buy it, recommend it to friends, buy one as a gift. When you're able to do that, you'll have found the place where good ads come from.

Or maybe you think good ads don't sell products any better than bad ones. So why try so hard to be conceptual? What's the big deal?

If you feel like that—and it would appear that you're not the only one—I have some bad news: you're trying (very hard) to get into the wrong business.

Make no mistake. Good ads sell products. (Good ads also win awards. But they win because they're good; they're not good because they win.)

And good ads help you get a good job.

You want to make good ads?

Think like a great shopper.

And do an ad that will convince my friend.

JEFFREY EPSTEIN IS THE FOUNDER AND DIRECTOR OF CHICAGO PORTFOLIO SCHOOL (WWW.CHICAGOPORTFOLIO. COM). HE STARTED TEACHING PORTFOLIO CLASSES AT THE SCHOOL OF VISUAL ARTS WHILE WORKING IN NEW YORK CITY AS A COPYWRITER AT TBWA AND SCALI MCCABE SLOVES, AND STARTED CHICAGO PORTFOLIO SCHOOL WHILE WORKING AS A CREATIVE DIRECTOR AT LEO BURNETT. CHECK OUT THE SCHOOL AT TWITTER.COM/ PORTFOLIOSCHOOL AND ON FACEBOOK.

FOR ONCE, IT *IS* ALL ABOUT YOU

BY GEORGE FELTON

Professor at Columbus College of Art & Design

Here's a true story:

One year, a senior created a portfolio with nothing in it but ads for skateboards, snack food, beer, and Doc Martens. He was snapped up by a good agency before school even let out.

Another student created a book with exactly the same mix. He's hauling furniture for a living.

What can we learn from this? "Life's a mystery" is one answer, and not a bad one. But another is that the mix of ads in your book doesn't matter as much as everyone says. We'd advised both students against narrowcasting a few of their favorite things, and you've heard that advice, too. I give it every year. But if you put your heart, your brains, and enough mojo into the work—as that first student did—you'll probably even be forgiven for a condom ad.

Another lesson? You can't really tell what an agency is looking for; maybe it's you. That first student, by accident, had created a book with an almost identical client list to the agency that hired him. They needed someone like him, and there he was. So cultivate a smiling persistence. Just keep knocking on doors and writing thank-you notes. I actually got this teaching position—not by sending out scores of applications, though I also did that—but by walking in the door to CCAD (Columbus College of Art and Design) when an English professor was walking out. Bingo. Despite our most careful planning, success can happen as simply as that.

Lap up all the advice you can get about putting your book together and finding that first job. Then chuck any of it that gets in your way. Think of rules as *suggestions*; that way, it's easier to shrug off all the contradictory advice you're getting.

Like this: Mark Fenske, when he visited CCAD, said that the only words he wanted to see in portfolios were those in the ads themselves: no descriptions of client, project, and purpose; no case studies; not even a résumé. The ads had to speak for themselves. If they mumbled, your tough luck. Luke Sullivan, when he looked at portfolios, told us just the opposite: he likes descriptions beside the work so he knows what he's looking at. If you're lucky enough to show your book to these two guys, you're going to irritate one of them.

Here's another damned-if-you-do, damned-if-you-don't decision: Should you take your own photographs for your ads, even if you're not a photo major? Plenty of excellent people say,

"Yes, absolutely." What better way to demonstrate your can-do attitude? But Joe Duffy, paging through a CCAD student's portfolio, wondered why anyone would make a creative director look at bad photographs. His advice: swap your skills with those of a photography-majoring classmate.

But swap skills often enough, and you arrive to this perplex: If all your ads come from team projects, how can a creative director tell where your talent leaves off and a classmate's begins? When I see the same projects in several books, as I often do, I begin to wonder whose thinking I'm looking at; I lose a sense of each book as an individual statement. You'll work in teams on the job, but right now you're just one person. Who, exactly, are you? With some books, it can be hard to tell.

All these contradictions from the best people in advertising and design have taught me that there are no rules, not really. At least there are a whole lot fewer rules than you think. So don't get tangled up trying to divine the mysteries of The Perfect Book. Try, simply, to be yourself.

Base each decision you make about a portfolio "rule" on who you really are at your best. Make that your one rule. It'll help you resolve all the other ones. Get past each perplexity the same way: what's the best thing for *you* to do?

So, for example, when you're pondering that descriptions-of-your-work perplex—should they be long, short, or nonexistent?—decide for *you*, based on your strengths. Can you (not your roommate or English-major friend) write strong, clear, crisp ones—or better yet, funny, revealing ones? Then write them, and let them go long if they sing. (Even though he says otherwise, Fenske will love you for them.) If your best words are unspoken—you're a designer, not a wordsmith—then make the descriptions short or leave them out.

Nothing in your portfolio is homework anymore; it's a measure of who you are and who you want to be. It's your first professional statement. Make it real and make it true. You can do that only by being yourself.

GEORGE FELTON IS PROFESSOR OF ENGLISH AT COLUMBUS COLLEGE OF ART & DESIGN IN OHIO, WHERE HE TEACHES DESIGN WRITING AND COPYWRITING. IN 2007, HE RECEIVED THE FIRST ANNUAL CCAD AWARD FOR TEACHING EXCELLENCE. HE IS THE AUTHOR OF *ADVERTISING: CONCEPT AND COPY*, NOW IN ITS SECOND EDITION, PUBLISHED BY W. W. NORTON.

REJOICE IN FAILURE

BY JACK FOSTER

Writer and former Creative Director

Here are five reasons why you should make failure a friend:

1. The only way to know that you've gone far enough is to go too far. And going too far is called failing.

But if you don't go far enough in searching for an idea—if you don't, in other words, fail—you can't be sure you've got the best idea.

So never fear failure or try to avoid it. Embrace it. Rejoice in it. It's a sign that you've gone far enough.

Race car drivers know this in their bones. They even have a saying about it: "The one sure way to find out if you're going fast enough is to crash."

Cooks know it too.

Nearly everything they make has an "Oops, we've gone too far" point to it.

And the only way they can learn where that point is, is to go past it.

So they learn not to burn rye toast or porterhouse steaks, not to oversauté chicken breasts or garlic or scallops, not to overmix whipping cream, or oversteam broccoli, or overwhip egg whites, not to overbake pork roasts or cakes or soufflés, not to...

The lessons are endless.

And the only way they can learn them irrevocably is by failing.

Emulate race car drivers and cooks.

Go too fast. Go too far. Let your mind wander into dangerous ground, into silliness, absurdity, stupidity, impossibility. Surprise your teachers. Astound your friends. Embarrass your parents. Thumb your nose at the laws of nature and science and common sense.

Crash.

Burn.

2. Ralph Price, an advertising agency art director I used to work with, says the same thing about failure: "You don't know if you've succeeded until you fail." But he meant something slightly different.

He meant that many times you don't know if an idea is any good until you have other ideas to compare it to.

That's why writers and art directors in advertising agencies come up with many ideas on every project they're working on.

I suggest you do the same thing on the problem you're working on. Once you come up with an idea that seems to work, put it aside. It won't go anywhere.

Then come up with another idea. And then another one. And the...

For as you will soon learn, if you haven't already, there's always another one. Always.

3. "I have not failed," Thomas Edison said. "I've just found 10,000 ways that won't work."

Emulate Edison. Put a positive spin on things when they don't work out. Believe that every failure brings you one step closer to success. It will prevent you, as it did Edison, from becoming discouraged. More, it will urge you on.

4. When you fail, it changes your mind set, the way you look at life.

Failing makes you fearless. Failing sets you free.

Perhaps Jerry Della Femina, the famous advertising man, said it best: "Failure is the mother of all creativity. My advice to anybody who wants to be creative is to get into something that will fail. I've failed at a lot of things in my life and I hope I fail at a lot more. Most people are afraid to fail, but once you've done it you find out it's not that terrible. There's a sense of freedom that you get from taking chances."

A friend of mine who was opening an office in Los Angeles for a major national advertising agency also knew this about failure. He was deluged with hundreds of applications.

"What kind of people are you looking to hire?" I asked him.

"The usual. Writers, art directors, account people, media, research—you know."

"But how do you choose, for example, one good media person from another?"

"I have to like them. If I don't like them, I won't hire them no matter how well qualified they are."

"What else?"

"I must confess, I'm partial to people who have failed."

"What?"

"People who have failed. They know that failure's never permanent; often, people who haven't failed at anything think failure's a disaster, and so they're afraid to go to the edge of what's possible. They're afraid to take chances. And because they've never failed, they think they know it all. I hate know-it-alls. Besides, you're always getting rejected in this business. That's just the way it is. I want people who I know will spring back."

The space program, so the story goes, felt this way too.

In selecting astronauts, legend has it that NASA looked for some evidence of failure in the résumés of the recruits. They knew that at some point in a space journey, the unexpected might happen—things might break down, not go as planned.

They wanted people who would not be unnerved by such a situation; people who had experienced failure before and had learned from it, become wiser and stronger from it; people who knew that failure is nothing but a temporary setback, a prelude to success, a door being opened, as well as a door being closed.

So don't hide your failures or be ashamed of them.

Wear them with pride. Revel in them.

5. Of course what I've been talking about are failures where you know things aren't working—crash-and-burn failures, failures that point you in another direction, failures that teach you something.

Every now and then, however, you know in your heart that your idea is a good one, that your solution will work if given the chance, that what you've done is right.

When that happens, use the failure as a motivation to keep trying.

The "I'll show them!" drive is a powerful vehicle. Ride it.

There are hundreds of stories about how this kind of stubborn refusal to accept failure eventually led to success.

Chester F. Carlson, inventor of the Xerox machine, spent seventeen years trying to get companies interested in his photocopying device.

Bette Nesmith Graham made her Liquid Paper (then called "Mistake Out") in her kitchen for a decade before it started to sell big.

Alfred Mosher Butts aggressively marketed his Scrabble game for four years before it caught on.

It took James Russell twenty years to convince the music industry to adopt his "digital music" invention.

Catch 22 was turned down by twenty-three publishers; Dr. Seuss by twenty-four; *Sister Carrie* by twenty-eight; *Chicken Soup for the Soul* by thirty-three; *Zen and the Art of Motorcycle Maintenance* by one hundred twenty-one.

Finally, if you'll allow me—a personal story of stubbornness:

Over a period of two years, I sent the original manuscript for this book to seventy-four publishers. Every time I got a rejection, I sent it out to a couple more publishers. The 44th one, Steven Piersanti of Berrett-Koehler, decided to publish it four months after I sent it to him. (While he was deciding, I sent it to thirty other publishers.)

Had I given up after getting forty-three rejections, there would not have been a first edition of *How to Get Ideas*, a book that has sold nearly 100,000 copies and been translated into fifteen languages.

Nor would you be reading this second edition now.

JACK FOSTER SPENT THIRTY-FIVE YEARS WORKING IN THE CREATIVE DEPARTMENTS OF MAJOR ADVERTISING AGENCIES; THE FIRST TEN AS A WRITER, THE LAST TWENTY-FIVE AS A CREATIVE DIRECTOR. HE HAS WON DOZENS OF ADVERTISING AWARDS, INCLUDING BEING NAMED "CREATIVE PERSON OF THE YEAR" BY THE LOS ANGELES CREATIVE CLUB. THIS ESSAY IS AN EXCEPT FROM JACK FOSTER'S BOOK, *HOW TO GET IDEAS*; REPRINTED WITH PERMISSION OF THE PUBLISHER. FROM *HOW TO GET IDEAS*, COPYRIGHT © 2007 BY JACK FOSTER, BERRETT-KOEHLER PUBLISHERS, INC., SAN FRANCISCO, CA. ALL RIGHTS RESERVED. WWW.BKCONNECTION.COM.

CLIFF'S NOTES

BY CLIFF FREEMAN

Chairman & Chief Creative Officer, Cliff Freeman & Partners

Thoughts about making it big in advertising:

Don't kid yourself.

You know great advertising when you see or hear it (if you don't, get out of the business immediately. But let's assume you do).

Great advertising is probably fresh and surprising in some way. It sounds different. It looks different. It has a different rhythm.

Apply these exact standards to evaluating your own work. If it doesn't cut it, give it the raspberry the way you would someone else's work.

Keep digging until you come up with something unique. And if you can't, tell your boss your work or ideas aren't great. At least not yet. That way you know that he knows that you know.

Write about the product.

In the greatest, soundest, most creative advertising, the theater always revolves around the product.

Ask yourself what makes the product "tick."

How does it fit into people's lives?

How does the competition fail or disappoint? What's its "personality" in the marketplace?

Advertising that isn't really about the product is almost always self-indulgent crap.

Don't be afraid to collaborate.

No one can do it alone.

There's a lot of talent out there.

Use it.

In the final analysis, the important thing is to be part of a great body of work.

Everybody's in the same boat.

Everybody—no matter how long they've been in the business, has those private moments of panic when they think they will never again come up with something great.

Everybody is constantly learning how to do it.

Every time you do a job, you learn something new—particularly in the area of film, when you're always confronting and (hopefully) conquering a new problem.

Stand for something.

This is a business where most clients are approving your work on faith. They must believe in you, so be consistent—never let your standards waver.

The power of advertising is awesome. More people will see your work than saw *Gone with the Wind*. You can shape society with it. It's a mind-boggling feeling. Enjoy it and good luck.

CLIFF FREEMAN IS ONE OF THIRTY-FOUR INDUCTEES TO THE ADVERTISING HALL OF FAME. ACCORDING TO A *USA TODAY* POLL, HE WROTE THE BEST COMMERCIAL OF THE TWENTIETH CENTURY ("WHERE'S THE BEEF?"). IN ANOTHER POLL CONDUCTED BY *USA TODAY*, IN CONJUNCTION WITH THE *4A'S* AND *ADVERTISING WEEK*, HE WROTE TWO OF THE FIVE BEST SLOGANS OF ALL TIME, ONE OF WHICH WAS "SOMETIMES YOU FEEL LIKE A NUT." HE IS THE CHAIRMAN AND CHIEF CREATIVE OFFICER OF CLIFF FREEMAN & PARTNERS, AN ADVERTISING AGENCY IN NEW YORK CITY. *CREATIVITY MAGAZINE* VOTED HIS AGENCY THE NUMBER ONE CREATIVE AGENCY IN THE WORLD THREE TIMES. MOST RECENTLY, CLIFF FREEMAN & PARTNERS CREATED THE "ICE CREAM AND CAKE" COMMERCIAL FOR CLIENT BASKIN-ROBBINS. AFTER ONE WEEK SALES WERE UP ON AVERAGE 40% AND THE CAMPAIGN WENT VIRAL WITH YOUTUBE HITS AT OVER A QUARTER OF A MILLION.

GETTING THE JOB YOU WANT

BY ROZ GOLDFARB

President, Roz Goldfarb Associates

Being in art school is the best time. It might seem like the worst time as you attempt to survive balancing your class load, work load, and private life. But, be assured, you will look back at this time in wonder at how much you knew and how little you knew.

Professionals are available for advice often telling you what is awaiting you "out there." I, for one, had zero career counseling, and no one ever told me about making a five-year plan or the need to determine a career path. Then again, I was a fine-arts major who couldn't spell or type, and a job wasn't in the plan.

Life doesn't always work on five-year plans. So here I am, head of a well-known recruiting firm, trained as a sculptor, wanting to be an art historian, and now dealing on a daily basis with literally hundreds of design firms and agencies clamoring for talent. What do they really want? And what do you want? Is there a match? Let's see.

What does it take?

Simply put, a passion for perfection and the recognition that the visual must have content and must respond to the marketing demands of the business climate.

You have to really, really want to do this and do it right, and you have to become pretty savvy about business.

Too many students and professionals try to get by through coasting. They rely on easy software solutions, stock houses, and other people's ideas. Taste is a factor, and a lot can be done with taste, smoke, and mirrors. But being eclectic is not the same as having a vision and being able to present it verbally. It takes a very special person who has the creative spark, who can visualize conceptual ideas and has the personal drive to sell the ideas.

The trap in this hypermedia culture is the speed with which new or trendy visual icons and images become average. Often it is the more experimental world of fine arts that can point the way toward new expressions, though newness is not always what drives something to be great.

I've always believed designers are the arbiters of taste, as they distill so much of our history and culture into a format widely distributed to the public.

Assuming I am right, you have a terrific opportunity and responsibility to contribute to our society.

What do they want?

"They," of course, are the enigmatic employers who make the big decisions on whom they are going to hire. What are they looking for? Mostly it can be summed up as issues of perceived talent, commitment, business savvy and "chemistry." Here are some guidelines:

The talent issue is very subjective, but it does rely on "vision" or having a point of view. It is amazing how a portfolio takes on the personality of the designer.

Creative people must be responsive to changing markets, and as I write this in 2009 the convergence as well as the multiplicity of media formats are making significant changes in the way people work. The integration of media is now producing the need for diversified flexible designers who can translate a brand to a host of channels. That ability to understand cross-channel marketing and apply ideas to various media is becoming essential.

Portfolios are always a personal statement and it is also interesting to note that students from the same school, and working on the same class projects, do not have the same portfolios. It is that hard-to-define personality that creates the separations and makes the differences. Content in design and advertising is a major factor.

One's ability to communicate the substance of the message—not to simply make something pretty—is a prerequisite. The creative use of typography not solely dependent on current software programs is very important. And, of course, everybody wants someone who can work hard.

Who gets the jobs?

I've just outlined some critical creative and human factors that employers throughout the country are seeking. However, it is the "chemistry" factor and, importantly, personal motivation that often clinches the deal.

The individuals who get the most sought-after positions in top firms are those who can communicate energy and enthusiasm for their chosen professions. You have to be articulate and well read, not only about the latest advertising and design buzz but about politics, business, and cultural issues.

You have to be a "people person," a team player who has the potential to lead the team some day. You also have to do your homework before an interview so you know as much about the firm as possible. Your portfolio got you this far, but now you have to sell yourself.

Employment is not only about your future but your future with the prospective employer. It's important to understand that senior-level creative people need to be good managers and are also part of the pitch process. They have to be prepared and able to make client presentations, be part of "selling" the solution and understand all sorts of economic contingencies as the apply to producing the work. When employers are hiring junior people they are thinking about the potential of this person and their potential future growth within the company.

How is the job market?

As I write this, the United States is in a deep recession, which has greatly effected the job market. As always, pendulums will move and things will improve. However, even in today's economy, the job market is full of new opportunities for creative people in all varieties of media. Global business expansion had driven companies to grow at an amazing rate, and while there is a retrenchment, there are benefits to people who can be flexible to their location and ready to relocate for the right position.

Our clients expect a great deal in ability and commitment, often complaining that the people are not good enough. What is good enough? Succinctly:

Creative freshness and innate intelligence.

Enthusiasm and passion for doing great work.

The potential to manage and present to clients.

I hope you will recognize these demanding criteria in yourself and truly be the future talent we all so definitely need.

ROZ GOLDFARB IS PRESIDENT OF ROZ GOLDFARB ASSOCIATES, A NEW YORK–BASED MANAGEMENT CONSULTING AND RECRUITING FIRM SPECIALIZING IN PLACEMENT OF CREATIVE, MARKETING, AND EXECUTIVE PERSONNEL FOR DESIGN, INTERACTIVE MEDIA, AND ADVERTISING.

HOW TO CONVINCE A CLIENT THAT THE WORK IS RIGHT

BY JEFF GOODBY

Co-Chairman, Goodby Silverstein & Partners

An agency is only as good as its finest work. No one sees or remembers the meetings, memos, and phone conversations that may have resulted in the denigration of a brilliant piece. By the same token, bad agencies often possess a file of solid work that they were simply unable to convince a client to run.

At Goodby, Silverstein & Partners, we are above all committed to the creation of great work. Therefore, when we are convinced that something is right, that it is truly a uniquely correct solution, we will do just about anything to explain and sell it.

We feel this way not for egotistical reasons, but for the benefit of our clients and their businesses. In the end, our clients retain us to guard the integrity of their marketing and advertising, to guide it intact through sometimes rocky political and legal waters.

It is in their interests that we hold strong opinions, that we push ourselves and the people around us because, as Pat Fallon says, *"The biggest mistake you can make is to spend all that money and find that no one even noticed."*

That said, it is important to add two things.

First, we are also deeply committed to the belief that a healthy advertising agency remains healthy and does its best work in the context of long, trusting client relationships.

This is a financial consideration, to be sure—but it is also a creative consideration.

Great campaigns don't just run for a month or two.

They acquire their depth and dimension over time. They prove their correctness in the marketplace and earn widespread respect, not just among creative people, but in the business community and in the public at large.

The trust that develops between agency and client can allow the advertising to take more chances, to truly stand for something, to obliterate the competition.

Second, we believe that work forced upon a client under great duress is a time bomb.

Such experiences greatly lessen the chances that we will be able to sell that client more, equally challenging work in the future. They lead to resentments that can bring a client to secretly hope that we—and the work we have forced upon them—will somehow fail.

Indeed, there are agencies that succeed through a succession of very short, stormy relationships that never really result in lasting, effective work for the client. For business and moral reasons, however, we don't intend to become one of them.

How, then, do we reconcile the need to sell great work with the demands of building long relationships? It is never clear and easy, but the following guidelines are key:

1. See things through the eyes of the client.
Look at yourself and your work from the client's standpoint, taking into account their business goals and personality. Is this the right work for them? If they are uncomfortable, is that discomfort something that can be overcome in time? Have you really addressed and discussed their needs? What have you done to earn or merit their respect?

2. Use trust, not force.
Trust results in an atmosphere in which you can do more, even better work in the future. You will have a client who roots for the advertising to succeed, even to the point of favorably interpreting research. Moreover, your life will be simpler, your stress lessened.

3. The client can be right.
Always remember that clients have thought about their businesses 24 hours a day for years on end. They are sometimes liable to know something you won't. Appropriate their instincts and knowledge as a solid starting point and don't be too quick to dismiss their perspective or ideas. In fact, don't be proud about adopting them whole cloth. Until you announce otherwise, the world will think the client's best ideas were really yours.

4. Avoid arrogance.
You probably have every reason to believe in your talent and perspective or you wouldn't be working here in the first place.
Yet there is a fine line that divides confidence and strength from arrogance. Confidence and strength make for long relationships in which severe differences of opinion can be constructively hashed out. Arrogance results in short term, often temporary gains, at best.

5. Create a partnership with the client.
If the client always sees you as an antagonist, you start every discussion with a disadvantage that must be made up in order to be successful. If the client sees you as a partner, half the job is done when you walk into the room.

Ed McCabe is one of the most cantankerous, opinionated, argumentative guys you'd ever want to meet. The clients he's done great work for are all well aware of this. Yet they consider him a friend with their best interests at heart.

6. Start over.

This may be the most important point here. The greatest enemy of brilliant work is the loss of perspective. As a piece of work undergoes long changes and revisions, it can often be transformed beyond recognition.

Before any of the participants know it, the very things that made it worth revising are dulled or gone. Be honest with yourself throughout this inevitable process. Is this still great work? If not, make your best appeal and then throw it away. (Sometimes the very act of offering this will galvanize a client to see the merit of your point of view.) It will be better for your work and the relationship. Besides, if there were only one way to do this stuff, it wouldn't be nearly as interesting.

JEFF GOODBY IS CO-CHAIRMAN, CREATIVE DIRECTOR OF GOODBY SILVERSTEIN & PARTNERS. HE IS A WRITER AND THINKER WHO HAPPENS TO WORK IN ADVERTISING. WITH PARTNER RICH SILVERSTEIN, HE HAS WON JUST ABOUT EVERY ADVERTISING PRIZE IMAGINABLE. *ADWEEK* CALLED HIM AMERICA'S BEST TELEVISION COPYWRITER, AND HE HAS BEEN CHOSEN THREE TIMES (ALONG WITH RICH SILVERSTEIN) AS *ADWEEK'S* CREATIVE DIRECTOR OF THE YEAR. HE HAS WON THE HOWARD GOSSAGE AWARD FOR BEST COPYWRITER FOUR TIMES.

GROW A PAIR

BY DEAN HACOHEN

EVP/Executive Creative Director, Cramer-Krasselt, Chicago

The key to a successful agency is mastering the art of listening.

Along the way, we learn plenty about strategy, concept, and execution. Even presentation.

But there's a far more basic skill that separates brilliant creative from decent ones: The art of shutting up and listening.

Mastering that art is not so much about common courtesy or respect. It's about the selfish need to find that elusive piece of gold: The trigger for a magical idea.

Keep in mind, I'm not talking about the hardware-winning idea you're going to come up with, I'm talking about the trigger.

It's there. Hidden in the weeds.

Sometimes it's buried in the brief. But more often, it's hiding in a far less obvious place.

Like in the middle of a focus group on a DVD nobody wants to watch.

Or in what a CEO says mid-sentence during a forgettable speech.

Or in five words from a junior account person that fall through the cracks in an internal meeting.

The insight. The angle. The way in.

Most people know how to listen. The trick is to "turbo-listen." Because even when our ears are peeled, we're usually only hearing half the answer.

I love the mantra of a longtime friend and colleague: "Listen to the words. But hear the music."

What's really being said between the lines?

Listening with big ears is easier said than done. Because some creatives have what another friend and colleague calls "small ears." That's a syndrome where stubbornness and pride shrink your eardrums to the point you may as well have no ears at all.

Small ears usually tilt good talent toward the wrong bull's-eye. Which leads to wasted time, and the bane of our careers: wasted work.

Of course, before you listen, you have to learn to simply shut up.

When we're so consumed with being heard ourselves, our brains can't process what there is to hear. Which can let a creative trigger slip through one ear and out the other.

And when you do hear it, remember it. Text it to yourself. Or go retro and write it down with an actual pen and piece of paper. It's scary how many insightful thoughts and clever ways of expressing them evaporate along the way because nobody pins them down. Kiss those gems good-bye.

Another benefit to listening with big ears: There isn't a client in the world that doesn't love it when a creative starts a presentation saying, "We heard you." If killer work isn't what they were expecting, but grounded in something you say you heard, you're more than halfway there.

Finally, acute listening is a skill that separates a good creative director from a sea of writers and art directors. If you're looking for ways to move up, use your ears wisely.

Listen, and listen well.

Because even though a great creative idea is rarely the result of doing what you're told, the ability to hear what you're told can unlock a great creative idea.

Here's to Q-tips.

DEAN HACOHEN HAS HELPED BUILD AND SHAPE CREATIVE AD AGENCIES FOR NEARLY THIRTY YEARS. HE'S GUIDED CREATIVE TEAMS TO CREATE AWARD-WINNING WORK FOR DOZENS OF U.S. AND GLOBAL CLIENTS, AND HAS WON AWARDS IN SHOWS AROUND THE WORLD. PRIOR TO HIS YEARS AS EXECUTIVE CREATIVE DIRECTOR AT LOWE IN NEW YORK AND AT INDEPENDENT CRAMER-KRASSELT IN CHICAGO, DEAN WAS A PARTNER AT LEGENDARY CREATIVE SHOP GOLDSMITH JEFFREY IN NEW YORK. ELECTED A VICE PRESIDENT OF DOYLE DANE BERNBACH AT AGE 27, DEAN BEGAN HIS CAREER AS A COPYWRITER AT WUNDERMAN. HE HAS SERVED ON THE BOARDS OF THE ONE CLUB AND THE ART DIRECTOR'S CLUB, AS WELL AS ON THE CREATIVE REVIEW BOARD OF THE AD COUNCIL. THIS ESSAY FIRST APPEARED IN *ONE. A MAGAZINE*; REPRINTED FROM *ONE. A MAGAZINE*, WITH PERMISSION OF YASH EGAMI; COPYRIGHT OF THE ONE CLUB.

DEAR PURPLES, PINKS, BLACKS, BROWNS, REDS, YELLOWS, GREENS, CURRIES, PERIWINKLES, TEALS, AND FUCHSIAS,

BY CHARLES HALL

Professor at VCU Brandcenter, Founder and Designer of Fat Daddy Loves You Bath Couture

if you want to be in advertising, design, branding, interactive, film or any of the other media and communication arts, there's only one thing to remember. don't be afraid.

don't be afraid of you. don't be afraid of them.
don't be afraid of the man, the man next to the man, or the boogie man.
don't be afraid to be aware of the lowered expectations for minorities.
don't be afraid not to take the free cheese.
don't be afraid to wear your heart on your sleeve. don't be afraid to feel things.

don't be afraid to win, succeed, compete.
don't be afraid to fail.
don't be afraid of criticism. don't be afraid of rejection. don't be afraid of the truth.
don't be afraid to ask for help. don't be afraid to not make excuses.
don't be afraid to party, laugh, dance, smell the roses, and drink the kool-aid.
don't be afraid to listen to your r&b, neo-soul, hip-hop, rap, jazz, rock, classical, punk, alternative, new wave, house, as loud as you like.

don't be afraid of institutional racism, sexism, homophobia, nationalism, or religious bias.
don't be afraid to not take it personally.
don't be afraid to express yourself.
don't be afraid of being the only one in the department, the meeting, on the set or under the gun.
don't be afraid of your beauty, your culture, your history, your strength, your identity. your vision. your story.

don't be afraid to see what is not being seen or to say what is not being said.

don't be afraid to listen, learn, grow, mature, adapt. adjust. excel.

don't be afraid of your talent.

don't be afraid to have a personality, a point of view, an opinion, a perspective, an objective and a positive attitude.

don't be afraid of words, lies, gossip, rumors.

don't be afraid to trust…somebody.

don't be afraid to be humble, thoughtful, considerate, collaborative.

don't be afraid of life, technology, emotions, passion.

don't be afraid of double standards.

don't be afraid of getting fired.

don't be afraid when they ignore you, slight you, forget to mention you or don't see you.

don't be afraid of cowards, liars, men with cronies, or false messiahs.

don't be afraid to play your "fuck-you" card.

don't be afraid to say it loud.

don't be afraid to be fabulous, ghetto, butch, spicy, holy, sexy, funky, ethnic, cultured, hard, educated, smart, strong, insightful, creative, better, you.

don't be afraid to flash your style, charm or intelligence.

don't be afraid to follow. don't be afraid to lead. don't be afraid to persevere.

don't be afraid to stand up for your friends. don't be afraid to stand up to your friends.

don't be afraid to stand your ground, speak your mind, and pay the consequences.

don't be afraid not to be the victim. don't be afraid to swallow your pride.

don't be afraid of those who are losing their head and blaming it on you. (thanks mr. kipling)

don't be afraid of those who are intimidated by you, uncomfortable around you, and insecure because of you.

don't be afraid to surrender, lose, fight.

don't be afraid to forgive, apologize, move on.

don't be afraid to own your mistakes, your bullshit, your fears, your faults, and your biases.

don't be afraid to take the chip off your shoulder.

don't be afraid to understand the difference between racism and power, sexism and chauvinism, homophobia and insecurity.

don't be afraid to think twice as fast, work twice as hard, sacrifice twice as much, and become twice as great.

don't be afraid to put people who look like you in your work.

don't be afraid to listen to your God, talk to your spirits, receive your blessings.

don't be afraid to pray.

don't be afraid when the odds are against you.

don't be afraid to take a risk and another risk and another risk and another…

don't be afraid to exhaust the possibilities.

don't be afraid to innovate and never assimilate.

don't be afraid to share and give and give and share and share and give some more.

don't be afraid to get more of this industry than this industry ever intended on giving…you.

don't be afraid to remember who you are, where you came from, and how you got here.

don't be afraid to not give away your power.

don't be afraid to believe…in yourself.

don't be afraid to out love them.

don't be afraid of history. don't be afraid of the future.

don't be afraid of today.

you can do this.

CHARLES HALL IS YOUR MIDNIGHT, CUPID, PIMP, PRESIDENT, LOVER, FIGHTER, LINEBACKER, POET, CHOCOLATE BUBBLE-BATH, SKINNY-DIPPIN', BON VIVANT, JESTER, PRINCE, CRAZY, DIFFICULT, HOPELESS-ROMANTIC, AWARD-WINNING, FAILURE, WRITER, DIRECTOR, CREATIVE DIRECTOR, BATH COUTURE DESIGNER, HUSBAND, FATHER, SON AND PROFESSOR AT THE VCU BRANDCENTER IN RICHMOND, VIRGINIA. HE HAS SPENT THE LAST TWENTY YEARS OF HIS LIFE AS A COMMERCIAL ARTIST AND LOOKS FORWARD TO SPENDING THE NEXT TWENTY YEARS AS A FINE ARTIST.

PART III: …A LITTLE HELP FROM SOME FRIENDS

NEVER STOP

BY JHAMES HOLLEY

Clergyman / Art Director

In 1999, I was hunting for my first job as an art director. At the time, nothing else in the world was more important than my quest for entry into advertising agency society. I remember the anxiety of planning trips that would present the best chance of meeting the people I needed to see.

Stressing over how to be myself without appearing to be too comfortable. Trying to decide what pieces stay in the book and what pieces come out.

These are some of the challenges many face at the pivotal point of graduating from an ad school and finding a job.

For you as a future creative star facing the same challenges, I offer advice. Not an answer, just advice. Once you've prepared yourself for the hunt, there is no formula.

You've studied advertising, crafted your skills, prepared a book and probably a Web site, and targeted several agencies.

There are many ways to open closed doors.

Some are obvious, others require persistence and wit.

Calvin Coolidge had this to say: "Nothing in the world can take the place of persistence. Talent will not; nothing is more common than unrewarded talent. Education alone will not; the world is full of educated failures. Persistence alone is omnipotent."

Being persistent is necessary in shopping your talent.

Two, maybe three, things make an impact on recruiters and creative directors. The first is your creative work.

Second is impressing them with your attitude.

Third is by someone recommending you. You'll miss opportunities for the second and third impact if you're not persistent.

With so many talented people knocking on agency doors, what is in your favor is that there are few people with good attitudes who are persistent and have excellent books.
What do I mean by persistence? Am I saying...

When you keep getting the secretary and she doesn't put you through, argue with her until she changes her mind?

When you wait in the reception area for an hour to be told to reschedule, burst into an office?

When someone says they have your book but they haven't looked at it, threaten to take it back?

No, no, and no.

With persistence there must be wit and tact.

Be nice to everyone, starting with the receptionist. If people think you deserve more courtesy, they will use their influence in your favor. Be persistently nice, not kissing up, but positive at all times. If you talk to agency personnel and they're in a bad mood, you have the chance to be the bright spot in their day.

Optimism in the face of adversity is underrated.

Accepting disappointment without being bitter can change people's opinion of you.

I'll share a story with you. I wanted to work at this one agency sooo bad. It was "THE agency" for me. The recruiter liked my book, but they weren't hiring.

How often is anyone hiring when you need a job?

Well, I asked one of my professors for his contacts at this agency. He gave me a name of a former student. I called the guy and set up an appointment. He looked at my book and was impressed. So I asked if he knew their creative recruiter. He said, "Yeah she's right down the hall, let's see if she has a minute."

In that situation she couldn't help but spend some time with me.

The meeting went well. My tactful path to her office amused her.

Maybe you've already experienced how tough it is just getting someone to return your phone calls.

Things go wrong, and at times life is a roller coaster ride.

With determination, you'll get through the low points.

I remember the mix of emotions I felt when news circulated around school about classmates getting hired.

I was happy for them, yet at the same time reminded that I must continue my search. This may happen to you.

If it does, use the success of others as inspiration.

Know that if there's a place in this business for them, there's a place for you. Persistence will lead you to that opportunity.

Being nice to everyone doesn't end with the agencies on your wish list. Yes, we all have a wish list.

Unfortunately everyone's list is often the same. What you're seeking is a position in advertising where you can gain experience and be mentored, not your dream job.

Many second- or third-tier agencies can be your key to opening a door at a first-tier agency.

Find your way to the ideal situation for yourself by establishing contacts. In my case, I made good contacts while freelancing at an agency that wasn't on anyone's wish list.

In fact, I met this agency's recruiter at a portfolio review.

Everyone else was battling in line to see people from the so-called hot shops. This recruiter was at a table by herself reading a magazine, and I was eager to show my book to anyone.

That meeting led to my freelance job, which paid for my trip to New York for interviews. The experience and friends I gained from that assignment opened doors at other agencies. This was a result of my respect for all levels of advertising, and persistence.

I remember what it was like to thirst for an opportunity to prove myself. It wasn't too long ago. You're asked to come back for one more person to look at your book before a decision is made.

You're told to wait a few weeks and see if they need to hire some people. Maybe a creative director tells you that your book is two campaigns away from "being there."

Still, no matter what ups and downs you face, be persistent.

Never stop making that extra phone call or visiting one more agency before you go home.

Never stop working on that one campaign that pushes your book to another level.

Never stop greeting interviewers with a smile and leaving their office with optimism.

Never stop, and remember that "nothing in the world can take the place of persistence."

SINCE EARNING HIS MASTER'S FROM THE VCU ADCENTER, JHAMES HOLLEY HAS PRODUCED AWARD-WINNING WORK AT LEO BURNETT FOR ALTOIDS AND ART.COM. HE HAS WORKED AT BURRELL ADVERTISING, PRODUCING TARGETED WORK FOR MCDONALD'S, PROCTOR & GAMBLE, TOYOTA, AND OTHER GLOBAL BRANDS. HE NOW FREE-LANCES AND IS THE PASTOR OF A CHURCH IN CHICAGO. YOU CAN CONTACT HIM AT JHAMESH@HOTMAIL.COM.

DO THE OBVIOUS

BY LEE KOVEL

Chief Creative Officer, Kovel/Fuller, Culver City, CA

Quite a few years ago, I was looking through some boxes in the back of a dust-filled antique shop and unearthed a small paperback booklet that was written around 1920. *Obvious Adams*.

It was the story of an advertising guy named Obvious Adams. As the story unfolded, Obvious got his start by meeting an ad biggie. At the time, Obvious was a clerk in a grocery store.

Now this ad biggie was quite preoccupied with one of his client's problems. Apparently, this client made biscuits. They were very good biscuits, too. They were sold by the pound right out of barrels. But sales, despite all the advertising, were not very good.

Obvious got into a discussion with the ad biggie and told him how the women he saw buying groceries always picked through the biscuit bin because many of the biscuits were broken. And he went on to suggest that maybe it would be a good idea if the biscuits were wrapped in their own containers.

The ad biggie thought this was a great idea (even though it was obvious) and immediately hired Obvious as a copywriter. And the client sold a hell of a lot of biscuits in the new packaging.

Now all through Obvious's career he did things that everybody looked at and said, "That's so obvious…why didn't I think of that?" But the catch was, nobody but Obvious thought of these things.

When you put your book together, there are often truths about products that other people miss. And if you look closely enough, you'll find them and the campaign idea will come.

Unfortunately, most books contain the same recycled thinking over and over and over. (Which is why you should go back to work on your book.)

For example, if you create work for eye drops, or toothpaste, or bug spray, look for the idea. Is there a relevant appeal that you can make that will coerce me into reading, clicking on, or watching and "relating" to what you're saying?

If you can't explain what the idea is, your advertising isn't working.

For writers, this is especially important. Banners, new media, viral, Web pages, copy, and layouts have to work together, too.

If you're an art director, your design skills may get you by in some remote cases, even if you get a B on the idea part. (Which is why you should go back to work on your book.) Now, more than ever, you must be adept at Flash, Dreamweaver, new media, retail, and even package design, and understand how it all flows cohesively to build sales and a brand. And you have to be able to create that old-school stuff like ads, brochures, and TV, as well. It's getting more complicated and more demanding. And bear in mind, I am using the word book interchangeably with your own Web site, computer presentation, and all the other ways to present yourself and demonstrate your training, knowledge, and your thinking.

In terms of good old-fashioned print, let me give you two of my favorite ads that illustrate ideas in print.

The first, for Parker Pens: "If the pen is mightier than the sword, then some pens are mightier than others." The visuals are a photo of Eisenhower holding the Parker pen used to sign the German surrender in 1945, one of MacArthur signing the Japanese surrender, and one of Warren Christopher signing the formal agreement with Iran to free 52 U.S. hostages.

The other ad shows a Range Rover going through a river with water up to its fenders. The headline: "We brake for fish."

The point is, there is a visual and verbal connection that makes these ads particularly good. And in most entry-level books there is rarely a connection like this.

If anything, there is simply a "punny" headline over a picture of the product. Don't do this.

Fill your book with ideas and with concepts that might even work across ALL media platforms . . . but remember, it is far from easy.

For Viral: what's relevant and cool and not selly. I like the Kobe leaping over the Aston Martin viral and the Ray Ban glasses getting tossed onto heads.

Now suppose you're talented enough to put together a body of work that can stand up to the best, which is highly improbable. (Which is why you should go back to work on your book.)

My next suggestion is to include some ideas that are controversial. Almost every creative director you meet will tell you to take risks.

Now, don't be stupid about this. Take smart risks. Your objective is to come up with advertising that makes people remember your book. That's right, the purpose is to make your book ever more distinctive. How long ago did Sasha Cohen appear at the Grammy Awards as Bruno? People remember the incident.

You see, every creative director worth his or her title is looking for young talent that can create the unexpected. Even if it's unsellable to a real client, a smattering of this in your book will help.

OK, so let's say your book is as good as you can make it...which is doubtful. (So go back and work on your book.)

The probability that you'll get a job is still slim. You simply have a great deal of competition for very few jobs.

As a result, you're going to have to go to work. You'll have to write letters and follow up with every contact you make. You might volunteer. Make your own "hiring" a low-risk deal for the agency. Think about an approach that might be new and compelling.

Of course, a great letter can be a powerful tool for getting a foot in the door. If you can't figure out what makes a letter great, advertising isn't for you. After all, direct mail is one of the purest forms of advertising.

But don't forget...99% of all creative directors will want to hire you because you have a superb book and show you ALSO understand how to create work in all media. You are better than a "print" writer...or a an "art director." Agencies are frugal, and if you can do many things well in terms of new media, viral, or maybe an event idea and STILL be conceptual, you rise to the top of the "maybe hire" list. The interview is a small, final hurdle. If your book is good enough, the interview is pro forma.

I'd suggest you pay attention in the interviewer because you may learn quite a bit.

First, you'll find most executive creative directors love to be intimidating in these situations to test your mettle. Take it easy. They're seeing if you listen, if you have conviction, and if you can talk.

Your book was good enough to get you face to face with the boss. Interview the interviewer. See what he likes (and hates) about your book. Listen carefully, because experienced people can help you make your book better.

You'll discover a lot about the way an agency operates by looking closely at the creative director. Should you get an offer, this is the person who sets the tone for the product and can make your life wonderful or miserable.

Keep your eyes open. Listen and learn. Don't ask stupid questions. (Then go back to work on your book.)

Finally, remember your book also reflects and brings your entire life experiences onto the page. The bits, facets, information, and all kinds of experiences you've had get stored subconsciously and reassembled into advertising.

Therefore, the more you know about a lot of things and the more you've experienced, the better your depth of bringing new ideas to bear. If you think this is a suggestion to work on a steamship bound for Tahiti, you're right.

Or you could work as a clerk in a grocery store. Both are relevant.

The vocabulary that makes great advertising stems from being able to arrange the right thoughts and images at the perfect time—so that people will respond. It's that simple.

Right now, you want to arrange your thinking and ideas to appeal to the people who will hire you: a dose of real-world ads, maybe some banners, some new media and one viral, some Web pages or things that might link together along with your mandatory brilliant print and TV—and a tight selection of off-the-wall "risk taking" ads.

You want that creative director to know you can sell mouthwash, cable TV, hamburgers, insurance, or bug spray better, smarter, in all media venues and more creatively than the hundreds of other people who are trying to sell mouthwash, hamburgers, insurance, or bug spray.

It's obvious, right?

Good luck.

And now, go back to work on your book.

LEE KOVEL WAS FORMALLY A CREATIVE DIRECTOR FOR YOUNG & RUBICAM NEW YORK, WHERE HE WORKED ON EVERYTHING FROM DR PEPPER TO JELL-O, AND WON FOUR CANNES LIONS. HE WORKED AT MCCANN NY ON MILLER LITE, CREATING SOME VERY FAMOUS WORK AND WAS EXECUTIVE CREATIVE DIRECTOR AT JWT NY, WHERE HE HIRED AND MANAGED A GROUP OF OVER A HUNDRED CREATIVE TALENTS. FOR TEN YEARS HE HAS BEEN PARTNER, OWNER, AND CHIEF CREATIVE OFFICER OF KOVEL/FULLER, A $150 MILLION CALIFORNIA AD AGENCY WITH A DOZEN COOL CLIENTS.

A PHONE OF YOUR OWN

BY LEORA MECHANIC

Copywriter, New York

Dear Secretaries/Would-Be Copywriters of America,

Don't throw in the towel! It can be done...I'm living proof!

We know, we know...you went to college and you can't believe you're sitting behind a desk saying, "Mr. Bosseroli's office" 47 times an hour. We know you hate it when everyone else is cc'd on memos and you're not because you're "just a secretary." Well, all that doesn't matter as long as you're working hard on your book, and you believe in yourself.

Actually, if you're serious about copywriting, then being a secretary (especially in the creative department of an ad agency) is much better than you think. That's what I did.

I guess I had a lot of gumption, gall, chutzpah (call it what you will), but I used to sprawl magic markers, magazine cut-outs, and headlines all over my desk. It was nice to have a lot of creatives roaming around so I could get their feedback—which is a blessing and a curse. When you show an ad to one person who loves it, feedback is great! However...one person's favorite campaign is another person's nightmare. After about ten months I decided if I really like the ad, it stayed in my book (like my DustBuster ad, which read, "This product really sucks.")

So where was I? Oh yeah...I was working on my book for a good eight months at Young & Rubicam. I made four-color copies of it and sent it out all over Manhattan.

What was nice about getting into the job search was that I learned something. After listening to all the hotshots in the industry, I realized my opinion really did count for something. This field is quite subjective, so at some point I had to follow my heart. Eventually it paid off.

After a year and a half at Y&R, David Metcalf (of Lowe Tucker Metcalf) called me and told me he liked my book. Given that I thought he was the best copywriter in town, I was considered at the time to be "thrilled to holy high heaven!" I met with him. He didn't want to hire a junior. I wept. He had no time to train. No money to spend. I convinced him it wouldn't cost him much. He wanted more experience.

I'll end this letter by telling you how I got the job (it may also be a juicy piece of advice). Are you ready? The reason I think I got my first copywriting job is because David liked my book. Period. He just needed that extra Push! I returned to work after our meeting and messengered him a thank-you letter that afternoon. I told him I would commit homicide to work at his agency. He hired me the next day. I was making the secretarial salary, but I was now a copywriter.

Six months later, a woman at McCann-Erickson called and asked if I'd be interested in writing radio and TV commercials for Coca-Cola. Does Dolly Parton sleep on her back?

Needless to say, I've been here for sixteen months and I'm enjoying myself. I get to be creative and use my musical ability, as well. Besides, I have a great secretary!

He wants to be a copywriter.

LEORA MECHANIC WROTE ADS AND JINGLES FOR COCA-COLA AND WROTE THIS TIMELESS PIECE BEFORE SECRETARIES WERE CALLED ASSISTANTS AND BEFORE WE ALL HAD THE E-MAIL MACHINE. HER POINTS ARE JUST AS VALID NOW. BE NICELY PERSISTENT. HAVE A GREAT BOOK. MRS. MECHANIC'S CREATIVE PURSUITS SHIFTED A FEW YEARS AGO FROM ADVERTISING TO SONGWRITING. SHE WRITES CHILDREN'S SONGS FOR THE EMMY AWARD–WINNING PBS TELEVISION SHOW "DITTYDOODLE WORKS." SHE IS THE SINGING VOICE OF LOLI. LEORA MECHANIC'S BUSINESS, "MEMORIES IN MOTION," DESIGNS CREATIVE MONTAGES FOR SPECIAL OCCASIONS.

SMART + BRAVE: WAKE UP EVERY MORNING WITH AN AWESOME AGENDA

BY DEBORAH MORRISON

Chambers Distinguished Professor of Advertising, University of Oregon, School of Journalism and Communication

You've heard this before: we live in changing times with evolving technology and emerging media shaping and re-shaping our profession. Throw in a few profound cultural shifts in politics, the economy, rampant globalization and you have a perfect storm happening to those trying to set sail in the advertising industry.

What you really want to think about though—I'm pretty sure of this after teaching for hundreds of years—is a simpler view of reality. How do I make the kind of book that gets me a first job? Better yet, how do I build a portfolio that sets the stage for my career in these crazy times? How do I create work I love?

The book you're reading has a few dozen great perspectives on doing that: how many pieces you need, how to build a network, smart ways to think about words and images that marry well, how and why the best in the business hire talent like you. What I want to offer is something a few left turns away from that straightforward talk. I'd like you to consider the big decisions about your life. And, ultimately, they all track back to answering those questions above.

1. Be brave. The industry and the world are full of timid souls who follow the crowd, adhere to protocol, never ask why. Enough of that. Your mantra to yourself should be to be courageous in your work. That might apply to simple things as in words and color and new approaches to media, or it might be broader. Maybe you challenge your own thinking on sustainable design. Maybe you look for a place to start your career in Ghana or Wales or Mumbai. Maybe you think about how your talent and skills can be used to solve the big issues of voter reform, health care, homelessness. The world needs your courage. Surely, this industry needs it also.

2. Be interesting. Interesting people are learners. They read, they observe, they question everything. Rachel Howald, one of the best in the business, is a group creative director at

McCann in New York. I remember watching her early in her career as she perused a music store and came up with a big find: the best speeches of the twentieth century on CD. To her, this was nirvana: language well-crafted and uplifting. She never ceases to surprise me with her eclectic collection of books, music, mementos. She continues to be one of the most interesting people I know because she is curious and uses it as a weapon.

Great creatives are curious at all costs. They don't stop at advertising. They live as anthropologists and social workers and storytellers and performance artists as they poke into areas that interest them. This serves two great purposes: their idea-making ability expands exponentially, and thus their careers blossom. More importantly, they are great to have a beer with. Great stories about how to make the perfect tapa, or the women's rights campaign in Saudi Arabia, or the perfect surf spot in Kauai. Interesting stuff.

3. Be indispensable. Loyalty and hard work often take a back seat to ego and credits in this business. The best writers and art directors usually have a sense that they need to work harder and smarter than others. That doesn't always equate to longer hours, but it does mean a couple of things about being productive. Be a good partner by being collaborative, honest, and inspirational. Be the person who's on top of meetings, by being prepared and on task. Know the custodial staff by name: this means you're staying late enough to get good work done and that you respect your office community. And even as writer or designer, you should know how to read and talk through a media plan or understand the real point of that latest RFP.

Being indispensable usually comes down to your colleagues trusting you to be remarkable on a regular basis. If everyone came into the office with this as their mission, wow…what a place that would be. Start the trend.

4. Be smart. Let's face it: this industry—especially the creative side—couldn't care less if you have a master's degree or a sixth-grade certificate. You're judged on your portfolio and your ability to keep the ideas flowing. So let's define smart in other ways. It means you back up your ideas with intellect and intuition. It means you make the most of any assignment thrown your way. It means you understand that a good idea doesn't live in seclusion, it is universally connected to other ideas and the people who have them.

Smart, my friends, means a junior book that is well-edited, surprising, and has something ownable in it. "I will want to meet—and probably hire—the person who shows me a book that is about being smart over being cocky, trendy, or too cool," a creative manager in San Francisco tells me. "I'll pass on a book that tries too hard. Or one that has obviously followed some template. I want to know I can throw this kid into a room of senior creatives and she will be articulate and add to the conversation. I can tell that by looking at her book."

5. Be good. There are parts of this industry that need you to be better than those already here. Give yourself and the world a reason to respect this profession. We need young talent ready to take on social issues, to reinvent the agency model, to use creativity as a world-changing tool for good as they help businesses grow. Look around at agencies dedicating their energies to social missions (Enviromedia in Austin and Portland, or egg in Seattle) or to lofty projects such as Hill Holliday's beautiful The Responsibility Project or Ogilvy's work for Dove. Use your talent to make the world better. Your careful sense of righteousness and responsibility should be put to good use.

Your book is about you and your take on the world. If you can prove to people through your work and your actions that you're brave, interesting, indispensable, smart, and good, you're in. Then write one of these essays and pay it forward.

DEBORAH MORRISON HAS BEEN TEACHING CREATIVE FOR A LONG TIME AT THE UNIVERSITY OF OREGON AND, BEFORE THAT, AT THE UNIVERSITY OF TEXAS AT AUSTIN. WITH BRETT ROBBS AS CO-AUTHOR, SHE WROTE *IDEA INDUSTRY: HOW TO CRACK THE ADVERTISING CAREER CODE* (ONE CLUB PUBLISHING, 2008). SHE AND GLENN GRIFFIN WROTE *PURE PROCESS: ADVERTISING'S TOP BRAINS REVEAL HOW BIG IDEAS ARE BORN* (F&W MEDIA, 2010).

WORDS TO LIVE BY

BY JIM MOUNTJOY

Executive Vice President/Creative Director LKM/Charlotte

I've always looked up to the legends of this business with lots of admiration and a hint of jealousy. Wow, what if I could do more great things like them? Their advice and wisdom have always helped me. But the best piece of advice I've gotten in ages came from an elderly lady sitting near a fountain in Rome one evening. She and her seven friends filled the square with such a happy laughter I couldn't resist greeting her, so I bought roses for the lot of them. They welcomed me to their table with hugs and we chatted. It turns out they are Holocaust survivors who became friends and meet once a year to remember and celebrate. I was speechless. As I began to leave I asked what advice they could give me. One hugged me and said into my ear, "Go live YOUR life."

DURING A THIRTY-PLUS YEAR CAREER SPENT SOLELY AT THE AGENCY BEARING HIS NAME, JIM MOUNTJOY HAS CONCEIVED AND PRODUCED A COPIOUS BODY OF WORK AND RECEIVED NUMEROUS NATIONAL AND INTERNATIONAL HONORS: THE ONE SHOW, THE NEW YORK ART DIRECTORS, COMMUNICATION ARTS, GRAPHIS, AND OTHERS. HE HAS TWICE BEEN NAMED BY ADWEEK AS THE SOUTHEAST'S TOP CREATIVE DIRECTOR. JIM HAS SERVED ON THE BOARD OF DIRECTORS FOR THE INTERNATIONAL ONE CLUB, AND CURRENTLY THE BOARD OF ADVISORS FOR THE CREATIVE CIRCUS AS WELL AS OTHER COLLEGES. THE UNIVERSITY OF NORTH CAROLINA NAMED JIM TO ITS HALL OF FAME FOR HIS CONTRIBUTIONS TO HIS PROFESSION, COMMUNITY, AND STATE. THIS ESSAY FIRST APPEARED IN ONE. A MAGAZINE; REPRINTED FROM ONE. A MAGAZINE, WITH PERMISSION OF YASH EGAMI; COPYRIGHT OF THE ONE CLUB.

STOP ADVERTISING

BY JAMES PATTERSON

Author and former Worldwide Creative Director, J. Walter Thompson Company, North America

How exactly do we make advertising that talks to people—to the way people really are, the way they really feel?

A strong case can be made for us to begin by *stopping* all advertising.

That is, advertising that looks and sounds like advertising.

That is, advertising that *imitates* the advertising of the past.

Let's begin with print. How do we make print advertising that doesn't look and sound like advertising?

I once had a very smart client who told me his idea of a powerful newspaper headline. The man was absolutely, positively brilliant in his perception about print.

The headline he chose—"Roosevelt Dies"

He offered another powerful headline—"Man Lands On Moon!"

Those sorts of headline are the competition our print advertising has in magazines and newspapers. The competition is news itself.

But headlines such as those also give us a feeling for the true power that is achievable on the printed page.

About TV.

I am personally uninterested in television commercials; I am especially uninterested in their subject matter.

I can't begin to describe my lack of interest in those primitive white-prints for TV commercials; those "storyboards" with nothing even faintly resembling a story, with neither beginning nor end, without plot; with the feeblest, stereotype characterizations—which keep appearing, day after day.

I tell the creators, and this is the absolute, honest-to-God truth, that I have no interest in iced tea made from a canned mix, in cars or any of their accoutrements, in removing plaque, in fast food burgers, in anything they have come to my door to sell.

In short, *I am the average consumer.*

I look at commercials out of the corner of my eye only.

Commercials have to come to me, not vice versa.

I try my damnedest to avoid, then to forget, every single TV commercial I see.

Nevertheless, I have found over the years, that certain tricks—certain "secrets"—employed by these creatives seem to work.

Here are some of those "secrets."

One. Be slaves to stimulus-response.

Make stimulus-response an automatic in the evaluation process. Evaluate everything in terms of these questions: What is the response we want? Is this the best way to get that response?

Two. Demand a cream pie in the face in every TV commercial.

I used to lie to the trainees every year.

I used to tell them I knew the secret of how to make $500,000 a year in advertising before they were thirty years old.

I told them—hit the consumer in the face with a cream pie—then, while you've got their attention—say something very intelligent.

If there is no cream pie in the ad, there is no ad. That's the truth…only it won't make you $500,000 a year. (The secret to making $500,000 a year before you're thirty is write trashy novels on the side.)

Three. All TV must be a poster—a sight poster; a sound poster.

The TV spot can have a hundred cuts, but the viewer must be able to take a single mind-poster away from it.

Four. Ask two questions over and over.

In the creating/evaluating process, you must constantly ask…

Who are you talking to—literally who?

What, exactly, is the response you want from them?

Five. Then, try to be intense about it.

Make them laugh, make them cry, make them sad, cute them to death, even insult them if nothing else works. Do something to them!

Because…

They don't want to hear your message.

They don't want to remember your message.

Once they turn on the TV, they are zombies!

Six. Design, craft, calculate.

Do it so that every frame, every word, every note works to elicit the response we want.

Seven. If even then, you're still not excited about shooting a spot, if you're not moved viscerally, kill it without mercy.

Finally, all writers of Irish descent must end each and every diatribe with…an Epiphany.

I guess it's about doing this thing, advertising, as well as it can possibly be done.

It's about having an honest work ethic, which demands that we make advertising that's better than any advertising before us.

It's about a way of life, a choice we make or don't make.

When I was a boy, in the summers I used to spend every Tuesday riding with my grandfather on his delivery route.

My grandfather had a deep, truly awful voice, and he used to *sing, every morning, at 5:30 A.M.* as he drove over the Storm King Mountains in upstate New York. He told me he really didn't care what I became when I grew up—the President, a ditch-digger—the only important thing was that I sang a happy song as I went over the mountain to work every morning.

And I do.

IN ADDITION TO HIS MAJOR RESPONSIBILITIES AS CHAIRMAN AND WORLDWIDE CREATIVE DIRECTOR OF JWT, JAMES PATTERSON WAS A LEADER IN THE SEARCH FOR NEW CREATIVE TALENT. HE MADE HIS MARK AT THE AGENCY WITH AWARD-WINNING CAMPAIGNS FOR KODAK, BURGER KING, TOYS R US, BELL ATLANTIC, AND MORE.

BUT HE'S PROBABLY BEST KNOWN AS ONE OF THE TOP-SELLING NOVELISTS IN THE WORLD TODAY. HIS DEBUT NOVEL, *THE THOMAS BERRYMAN NUMBER*, WAS PUBLISHED WHEN HE WAS TWENTY-SEVEN, AFTER HAVING BEEN TURNED DOWN BY MORE THAN TWO DOZEN OTHER PUBLISHERS. HE HAS SINCE WRITTEN FIFTY MAJOR NATIONAL BESTSELLERS AND COUNTING, WITH AS MANY AS NEW NINE NEW NOVELS COMING OUT EVERY YEAR, ALWAYS AT THE TOP OF THE *NEW YORK TIMES* BESTSELLER LIST. AT THIS WRITING, ONE OUT OF EVERY FIFTEEN BOOKS PUBLISHED IN THE UNITED STATES IS BY JAMES PATTERSON.

HOW TO BECOME GOOD AT ADVERTISING: ONE PERSON'S POINT OF VIEW

BY ROBIN RAJ

Citizen Group, San Francisco

So how exactly does one become "creative?"

What makes one ad brilliant and another seem like a walking strategy statement?

The answer to these Zen-like questions could fill a book.

Apparently, they have. The only advice I might give anyone starting in this business is this: Don't just develop your portfolio. Start developing your point of view. A way of seeing things and expressing things that has a piece of you in it. It's never too early.

In the end, it's all any creative person in this business gets paid to do—offer a fresh perspective. At a moment's notice, you may be called to draw upon the dramatic, the fantastic, the useful, the sarcastic, the absurd.

So it follows that the broader your sensibilities, the better you'll be. It's been my experience that some of the best people in this business never consciously set out to be in it. Instead, they brought with them a wide range of not-necessarily-related experiences. And were better for it.

Every good ad person needs to be a student of the culture—past, present, and future. And the more you feed your consciousness, the more your subconscious will feed you.

Here are some obvious places to begin.

1. Start a file. Archive the ads or content you admire. Then ask yourself, "Why?" The goal isn't so much to emulate others, but rather to appreciate the thinking that was put in. See? You do have a point of view.

2. Read and write. Of the three R's, the first two are inseparable if you plan to make a career of communication. Devour as much as you can—books, magazines, whatever. (Try this: for every article you're interested in, read one you're not.) Then devote time to composing your own thoughts. All media—linear or non-linear—is rooted in storytelling. Tell us a story.

3. Just do it. If you have the chance to visit Rio, or go to a rodeo, or watch a Fellini film, go there. Nothing beats personal experience and new experiences. It may be the grandest rationale of all for goofing off.

4. Art directors, force yourself to think verbally. Writers, force yourself to look at the world visually. Become conversant with both languages, and you'll become more than twice as valuable.

5. Go wide and deep. Interactive media changes things only completely. It's a chance to think far more dimensionally about how best to tell your story, and deliver information, education, and entertainment beyond the constraints of 30 seconds. Who can't get excited about that?

6. Know your audience. Not just in some generalized "demographic" sense, but as people with flesh and bones. Talk to them. Ask them questions. And then, as you write, speak with them one-on-one across the table.

7. Make it all work together. Today, everything is media—for better or worse. Consider what media is appropriate to deliver your idea. Then consider all the moving parts of a campaign and how they work together. Today's creative person needs to think as much like an architect as they do as a storyteller.

8. Become a student of advertising history. See what others have done before you. Learn to appreciate it, and then learn to defy it. Just because it's in an award annual doesn't mean it's enshrined. Or that you can't do better.

9. The ethical imperative. With issues like climate change and health care facing us, in my opinion ad people can no longer afford to think narrowly about their role in the world. Your innocent and well-intentioned ad will be seen by millions. Think about it. And take responsibility for what you sell.

10. Be selective about where you want to work. Ironically, this may be the best time of all for you to guide your career—before you're conforming to someone else's expectations. Make a short list of agencies you respect. And pursue them with a passion.

11. Perhaps the hardest lesson of all—learn to be patient. Great ideas sometimes happen on the first try, but not often enough. Develop the resilience to go beyond your last idea until you have something both your heart and head can't ignore. Who knows? You might have solved the problem.

12. Remember, no one in advertising ever stops learning. Unless, of course, they retire. If you enjoy the process, you probably chose well. Advertising sure could use you.

ROBIN RAJ IS BEST KNOWN FOR HIS IMAGINE CAMPAIGN FOR AMNESTY INTERNATIONAL, WHICH RAN IN MORE THAN SIXTY-FIVE COUNTRIES, AND AS THE WRITER OF THE NYNEX YELLOW PAGES CAMPAIGN, WHICH THE ONE SHOW VOTED "ONE OF THE TEN BEST CAMPAIGNS OF THE PAST 25 YEARS."

NO, REALLY, I LOVE IT. I'VE ALWAYS WANTED A JUMBO PENCIL WITH A TROLL ON THE END

BY AMY KROUSE ROSENTHAL

Author and host of *Writer's Block Party* on WBEZ Chicago Public Radio

"Nothing compares with the paperweight as a bad gift. To me, there is no better way than a paperweight to express to someone, 'I refuse to put any thought into this at all.'"—Jerry Seinfeld

There's so much dreck out there. I'm not just talking about "bad" advertising. But stupid movies; lobotomy-compatible TV; honking taxis; mean, icky people. There's no escape. It's like the game dodgeball you played in the fifth grade. You'd run. You'd duck. But somehow you always ended up getting smacked across the face.

Now think about how refreshing it is when you see a movie you can't stop playing over in your mind. Or read a cartoon that makes you rip it out and tape it to your wall. Or you're three cents short and a stranger in line just hands it to you.

Or see a commercial that assumes you have a brain.

The respected designer Rick Valicenti once said to me, *"We're in the business of giving gifts."* That is exactly what these rare moments are: Gifts. A little gem in the middle of an otherwise blah-filled day. It feels great. You appreciate it. You *remember* it.

Instead of asking ourselves the same, unanswerable questions—"Is this ad good?" "Will it break through?" "Will the client like it?"—maybe we should be asking, "Is this ad a *gift*?" "Will it change someone's life for the better?" "Is it something I would want to receive myself?" Or is it a case of "I sure as hell don't want this, but I think I'll wrap it up again real nice and unload it on someone else."

As we all know, making a big production out of the wrapping paper doesn't make a dumb gift any more desirable.

Creating this kind of meaningful advertising takes a fair amount of generosity and honesty. Take a step back from it. Have you created something the other person (the consumer) truly wants? Or just something you want? Or the client wants?

It's like dreams.

I believe dreams are phenomenally intriguing, but only to the person who had them. Other people's dreams are boring. With a capital Zzzzzz. "It was so weird. We were in this field, there was this guy and all these little cucumbers, and then…" Likewise, the story of the specially formulated thingamajig is truly interesting to the advertiser, but the consumer couldn't care less.

I'm looking at a package of Pepperidge Farm cookies. On the side is an illustration showing how a man looks in a well-tailored suit versus a poorly tailored one. The caption says, "This has absolutely nothing to do with Pepperidge Farm cookies." I love that. Instead of boring me with how scrumptiously scrumptious their cookies are, they charmed me with their silliness. I'm left thinking, "What a cookie company. You made me smile. Here, take my money."

And here's a standard fax cover sheet. What could be interesting about that? I quote, from the bottom of a Mad Dogs and Englishmen fax, "If you experience trouble with this transmission, it's probably not our machine…we got the deluxe model." I bet their clients smile and think, "That's *exactly* why we hired them!"

If the smallest, most mundane pieces of communication can be turned into gifts, what's our excuse with thirty seconds or a two-page spread?

The Aztecs would have been great at advertising.

When the sun set each night, they were terrified it wouldn't rise again in the morning; they were extraordinarily grateful for every dawn. So I bet the Aztec Ad Chief would have approached each assignment thinking, "We'd better do something special here; this may be our last chance."

We're really lucky—as the creators and purveyors of advertising, we have countless opportunities to really do something special. We're given all these blank spaces, and what we fill them with affects a ton of people. It would be so much nicer—and much more—to tap the consumer on the shoulder and say, "Here, this is for you, I want you to have this gift."

AMY KROUSE ROSENTHAL STARTED HER CAREER AT GOODBY SILVERSTEIN & PARTNERS, THEN MOVED ON TO WHAT SHE CALLS, "A VERY HAPPY TEN-YEAR CAREER IN ADVERTISING." SHE NOW WRITES BOOKS, MAKES FILMS, AND HOSTS A RADIO SHOW. SHE LIVES IN CHICAGO AND RESIDES CYBERLY AT WHOISAMY.WORDPRESS.COM. THIS ARTICLE ORIGINALLY APPEARED IN *ADWEEK*, USED WITH PERMISSION OF E5 GLOBAL MEDIA, LLC.

WHY A BOOK ISN'T A BOOK ANYMORE

BY HELEN KLEIN ROSS

Digital storyteller and author of AdBroad blog

When I broke into the business, it was a different business. Copy was mailed to a client, with stamps. Art directors could draw. Cut and paste called for blades and rubber cement.

But you? You're coming into advertising in the throes of a maelstrom. Long-held rules of marketing are changing and ad agencies are going through gyrations trying to keep up. Creative directors are scrambling to retrain their staffs, to figure out how to stake claim for brands in the new, digital world. A few years ago, "doing interactive" meant coming up with banner ads. But Web 2.0 has made the medium more challenging and creative directors are hoping that you, the first generation of digital natives, will come up with brilliant ideas for exploiting it.

Don't get me wrong. To get a job in advertising, you still have prove your creative prowess in print and TV. But now every concept also needs a digital component that shows you understand the shift to conversational marketing. The ideas that are most likely to land you a job are ones that promote brands across multiple platforms: print ,TV, Facebook, Twitter, or whatever is the latest application du jour.

That's why the best way to show your book isn't a book. It's a Web site. Claim your name (or some variation) in a URL and create a case for yourself on the Web. Once your work is online, creative directors can look at it whenever, wherever they please. And a digital "book" has the added advantage of never getting lost or tying up your chances at an agency because another agency, after three weeks, still hasn't gotten around to looking at it.

Your Web site doesn't have to be fancy. In fact, it's a good idea to keep it as simple as possible. Creative directors are looking to assess your concepts, not your mastery of widgets and code. They won't take kindly to being made to wait, no matter how cool your site is when the Flash finally loads. They make time for your work and you make your site so heavy they have to stand by for the loading bar? You've just demonstrated a cardinal sin in advertising—not knowing your target. Click. Through.

What else?

1. Make a list of where you want to work. This may sound basic, but I'm always surprised by people who don't think to do this. Look for agencies instead of job offers. Where you start in the business is the most important career choice you'll make, as the connections you form there will help determine the jobs you'll get next. Success in advertising, as in most businesses, depends partly on who you know and who knows you.

2. Know the good campaigns. What won awards last year? Which do you admire? This is a common question in interviews and answering it gives a creative director an idea of what *you* think is good, and if it dovetails with her own ideas. Don't go to an interview without having an opinion or two about what kind of work you're seeking to emulate.

3. Read the ad blogs. They're a great source of what campaigns are being talked about now, what it's like to work in an ad agency, even what to wear on your first day at work. There are lots of blogs to choose from. *AdAge*'s Power 150 is actually list of over 900 blogs, each appealing to a slightly different sensibility.

4. Read the trades. *Adweek. AdAge. BrandWeek.* Doing so will feed your head in a way that sets you apart from most applicants who limit themselves to *Creativity* and *Campaign*. (Which you should read, too.) Remember. Advertising is an art, but it's also a business. Creative isn't creative if it doesn't sell.

5. Clean up your Facebook. Google your name. See what comes up. Is that something you want prospective employers to see? Trash those photos of spring break when you were a sophomore. Get a LinkedIn profile. Take yourself seriously. Until you do, nobody else will.

HELEN KLEIN ROSS STARTED OUT AS A SECRETARY TYPING COPY FOR REAL-LIFE MAD MEN, SPENT TWENTY-PLUS YEARS AS A WRITER/CREATIVE DIRECTOR IN NEW YORK, THEN SEGUED INTO SOCIAL MEDIA, WHERE SHE IS @ADBROAD AND @BETTYDRAPER ON TWITTER. SHE IS AN AVID SPEAKER ON TWITTERTAINMENT AND FOUNDED BRAND FICTION FACTORY TO LEVERAGE NARRATIVE FOR CONSUMERS IN THE DIGITAL SPACE.

ONCE UPON A TIME

BY RON SEICHRIST

Founder and Global Director, Miami Ad School

I'm not young anymore.

I was young in the 1940s when my family would sit around a stare at the radio and listen to *The Shadow* and *Fibber McGee and Molly*. The commercials for Johnson Wax were blended into the program as part of the story.

I was young in the '50s. Back when layouts were done with pastels and paints, by people who could indicate with exquisite precision 10-point type with a camel's-hair brush. I remember the magic marker revolution that put the pastel wrists to pasture with layouts that always looked better than the printed ads. And I remember the Letraset/Xerox revolution.

I watched black and white television turn to color and replace the creative directors who could only think in Print.

I was also still around for the computer revolution a few years ago. And what a marvelous revolution it was. After so many years, the end of portfolios as we knew them.

I remember portfolios. You know, those black imitation leather cases that held students' inkjet comps of print ads and TV storyboards. Remember those? For a nanosecond the portfolios were replaced by CDs and DVDs. Now it's all about links. Paper is passe; ink is out. Digital über alles.

From your doctor's office to the gasoline pump, our whole universe is now dominated by flat panel TVs; your iPhone and iPod are all touchscreen; by Christmas so will most of the television screens be touch magic until they are replaced the following Christmas by voice recognition; I just bought a 70-inch touchscreen TV with built-in Internet for my living room; vending machines talk to you while taking your video to post on YouTube; newspapers are dying and born again on your mobile; giant billboards are digital and advertise caffeine-rich coffee on the drive in to work and caffeine-free coffee on the way home; my daughter texts me to tell me she liked the lunch I packed and she texts me from her digital camera; her thumbs fly a hundred miles an hour while I peck with the side of one finger at the very small keys; my text is more hieroglyphic than English; we now teach classes at Miami Ad School where the art directors in Madrid are teamed with copywriters in San Francisco and the teacher is in New York City, all connected by our global telepresence system; in between classes they chat by Skype.

But I'm from the past and all this technology and social networking is mind-numbing for an elder like me. What's the Ad World coming to anyway? What's the future going to look like?

Well, I found out this summer. The future is going to look an awful lot like the past. Can I tell you a story about how I discovered this remarkable insight?

It began in July. I invited five of my second quarter copywriting students to join us at our farm in the middle of the mountains in North Georgia. We spend a good part of the summer quarter there but stay in close contact to Miami and our other schools by our video presence system. The students took classes with me in basic photography and wordsmithing. We met every day and had intensive writing and photography sessions and they made great progress. After a few weeks it was time for the students to go back to Miami. But two of them asked if they could stay longer and would I please give them a giant, very challenging project. Sure, why not? It would be fun.

I told them that our land had been a part of the Cherokee Indian Nation back before the Trail of Tears. The locals talk about the Indian spirits that still haunt the area. So I asked the students to write and photograph something about the Cherokee spirits. They jumped on the project. We all took a 30-minute trip to Cherokee, NC, where we visited the Cherokee Museum, visited the Indian village, and went to the Cherokee outdoor drama. We learned about their culture, their spiritual lives and their legends, particularly the importance of the "Storyteller." The Storyteller passed on the Cherokee history from generation to generation. And the students knew they must tell the story of the Storyteller.

We came back to the farm and made Indian masks, spears, and Indian garb.

At night the students photographed each other (and our kids) as Indian spirits. They lit the images by flashlight, spotlights, and car headlights at all-night-long photos shoots, throwing smoke bombs into campfires, often under 200-foot waterfalls. During the daylight hours they wrote stories paralleling the Cherokee legends. They gathered all these words and photographic images, put them into their computer, created a little more Photoshop magic and published their books from the online publisher Blurb, and had hardbound books in a few days.

The result was beautiful, powerful. And it was an amalgamation of past, present, and future. The way it has always been. We continue our history with stories; we look to our future with stories; we revere our Storytellers. Now we have the technology to make our stories come to life—to hear the sounds, to re-create any event, to make any alien or monster as real as the dog on our lap.

Now more than ever, we need the Storytellers. And we need them more than ever in advertising. This then, was my revelation: the more we change, the more we stay the same.

Creativity for all of us actually begins with, "Tell me a story, Daddy." And before you know it we're shooting films, writing blogs, designing graphic novels, and making ads.

SIMPLICITY WITH VISUAL IMPACT

THIS ESSAY, ALSO WRITTEN BY RON SEICHRIST, FIRST APPEARED IN A PUBLICATION BY THE MIAMI AD SCHOOL, *TOP DOG: TIPS ON PRODUCING AWARD-WINNING STUDENT WORK AND A JOB-WINNING PORTFOLIO*, REPRINTED, HERE WITH THEIR PERMISSION.

Simplicity. KISS. Keep it simple, stupid. The visual solution, thank you. Who has time to read? Who does read, anymore? Just clear, to-the-point communication. Life is short as it is. Besides, if you want to know products and benefits, go to the Internet and read all about it. But, for print ads, let's make it simple. Powerful images with lasting impact. Close-ups. Even closer. Try to make it funny. Outrageous. Over-the-edge. Remarkably, the one-two punch of the camera and the computer has given the students tools so professional, student work can be as professional as the professional. And if the professional was born before 1973, his work will be sloppy compared to today's kid who grew up with Sony Playstation and XBox. It's all visual these days. If there is a headline, usually the type size requires a magnifying glass. No body copy whatsoever. Mostly, there's just a tagline. But the photos and illustrations in the ads are magnificent. Mouth-watering, hair-curling, and groin-tickling. In such an environment we give the following advice to our art direction students. Shun stock photographs whenever possible. Fall in love with the camera. Learn all you can about photographic lighting. Study the great masters of photography. But haunt all the art galleries as well. Take up "tagging" or whatever it's called today. Collect hand-made signs. Take a Play-Doh class with second-grade kids. Take up taxidermy; maybe you'll put together a bull-frog band for a music campaign. Enroll in a Japanese calligraphy course. Collect hand-carved tombstones. Go to a flea market and collect Ninja Turtle stuff. Ask your grandmother for her old photographs. Talk your grandfather out of his early pornography. In other words, collect solutions now for problems you're going to have some day in the future. Become one giant reservoir of useless, but interesting, trivia.

RON SEICHRIST IS THE FOUNDER OF THE MIAMI AD SCHOOL, WHICH NOW HAS FULL-TIME SCHOOLS IN MIAMI, MADRID, MINNEAPOLIS, SAN FRANCISCO, HAMBURG, BERLIN, AND SAO PAULO, WITH NEW YORK AND BEIJING TO COME. IN 1979, SEICHRIST FOUNDED THE PORTFOLIO CENTER, THE FIRST PORTFOLIO SCHOOL IN THE UNITED STATES. SEICHRIST WAS CHOSEN BY *ADWEEK* AS ONE OF THE TEN PEOPLE WHO SHAPED ADVERTISING IN THE LAST DECADE. THE NEW YORK ART DIRECTORS CLUB HAS ALSO PRESENTED HIM WITH A GRAND MASTER OF EDUCATION AWARD.

HOW TO LOVE PACKAGED GOODS ADVERTISING

BY SUSAN SPIEGEL SOLOVAY

Creative Director, BrandVisioning.com, former Senior VP, Group Creative Director, Grey Advertising, New York

I don't know about you, but I can easily spend the afternoon in a drugstore, buying a shampoo. Probably because I get lost in the siren song of the hand-lotion aisle first, certain that "Now with Aloe" spells the miraculous end to my dry hands.

Then I might spend a quick half-hour choosing, say, a dental floss flavor and width. I steal a moment for lip gloss to make my lips look wet and talc to make my toes feel dry.

It's exhilarating! I leave the store with armfuls of promise. And some of these products really do make me feel terrific. And the others? Well, I've wasted a few bucks on the thrill, but it's cheaper than Atlantic City, with slightly better odds.

Maybe this is why I've always found it easy to work on packaged goods assignments. I understand that brands "talk" to you from their perch on the shelf.

They promise to make you feel just a little better with them than you did without.

And the brand's impression is built from all the words and images you've stored up about the product. The name, the package, the TV commercials, the people in the ads, maybe a song, a sound, a color; maybe a fleeting image, a set of words—it's all so quick, I doubt many people are aware of it.

As an artist and writer, what a delicious job it is to help form that impression!

What's more, it's not as hard as some people would have you think. You just have to love your product. Then it's awfully simple to get other people to love it too.

That's why, when you're starting a portfolio, take Maxine's advice. Start from what you know and love. If you find it hard to get enthused, start considering another line of work.

Because once you've got a job, you don't get to choose your product assignments from your own bathroom or kitchen cabinets.

That's when you learn to be unashamed about learning why other people use the products they use.

There is always a reason. That's one of the beauties of advertising. People don't part with their money without a reason. You can't make people buy things they don't feel they need.

Hold on, you say. (I know your next question. I've been teaching advertising classes for years.) Aren't there a lot of useless products out there? What do you do when you have to work on something you think is boring?

Well, in the grand scheme of things, some products really do seem useless. I mean, did the world really need "2,000 Flushes"? Or a new scent of carpet freshener?

The answer is: *You* may not need it, but someone else does.

Otherwise the company that made it would not have bothered. In the best of all worlds, manufacturers look for unmet consumer needs before inventing products to fit those needs.

And the second answer is: You work on it just like anything else you do. You learn to love it. Become the person who needs it.

Wear their shoes for a while. And then turn your insights into the brightest, most impactful communication you can.

So you can stop people, and reach them with your wonderful promise. Whatever it may be.

As long as there's someone who needs to know that Crest fights cavities better, or that Clorox smells lemony now, or that Sure keeps you drier, and Olay keeps you moister—as long as there's a product with a promise, there're going to be people like me filling pages up with ideas of how to tell the world about it.

And I'm going to be having a lot of fun doing it.

SUSAN SPIEGEL SOLOVAY HAS MADE A CAREER OF WINNING AWARDS ON PACKAGED GOODS ASSIGNMENTS THAT MOST PEOPLE WOULD RUN FROM. SHE CO-CREATED WELL-KNOWN CAMPAIGNS LIKE "THE BEST PART OF WAKING UP IS FOLGER'S IN YOUR CUP" AND "SURE/UNSURE," AND UPDATED AGE-OLD BRANDS LIKE JIF PEANUT BUTTER AND DOWNY FABRIC SOFTENER. RECENTLY SHE CO-CREATED BRANDVISIONING TO HELP AGENCIES AND CLIENT COMPANIES "DEEP DIVE" INTO THE SUBCONSCIOUS MIND OF THE CONSUMER USING "WHOLE BRAIN" TECHNOLOGIES LIKE HYPNOSIS AND GUIDED RELAXATION (BRANDVISIONING.COM).

THINK BIG

BY HELAYNE SPIVAK

Legendary Creative Talent, NYC

Let's face it. Most Web sites are boring. Most television commercials are playing it safe. And magazines are closing as page by page print advertising is disappearing. So, what does that mean? We have to think bigger on every level.

Brand news used spread by frequently running ads. Now, if your idea is fresh enough or impactful enough or outrageously funny enough—it's picked up and spread by your consumers. This is good news.

The advantage for anyone starting out today is that the sky is, literally, the limit…as long as the brand is still the focus.

Want to promote female self esteem by plastering naked women of every age and size on billboards all across New York City? Dove did.

Think it would be a cool idea to take Whoppers off the menu at Burger King and see what people's reactions would be? Burger King agreed.

Think it would be hysterical to have a guy come out and tell you exactly what parts of his body he shaves (in disturbing detail)? Philips Norelco said, Let's do it.

The challenge today is not simply to find the way to sell a brand, it's to fully explore every way.

So the best advice I can offer is this: if you want to do work that gets word of mouth, give them something to talk about.

HELAYNE SPIVAK HAS WON EVERY MAJOR AWARD THE ADVERTISING INDUSTRY OFFERS, INCLUDING THE PRESTIGIOUS MATRIX AWARD FOR WOMEN IN COMMUNICATIONS. HER STORIED CAREER INCLUDES TIME SPENT AS CHIEF CREATIVE OFFICE OF Y&R AND JWT. PERHAPS SHE WILL TELL YOU THE STORIES SOMETIME. SHE TAUGHT COPYWRITING AT THE SCHOOL OF VISUAL ARTS AND THE MIAMI AD SCHOOL, AND IS CURRENTLY CHIEF CREATIVE OFFICER OF SAATCHI & SAATCHI WELLNESS.

THE GOSPEL ACCORDING TO LUKE

BY LUKE SULLIVAN

Managing Group Creative Director, GSD&M in Austin, Texas

Get to know your client's business as well as you can.

Bill Bernbach said, "The magic is in the product. You've got to live with your product. You've got to get steeped in it. You've got to get saturated with it."

Your clients are going to trust you more if you can talk to them about *their* industry in their terms. They'll quickly find you boring or irrelevant if all you can speak about with authority is Century Italic. Your grasp of the client's marketing situation has to be as well-versed as any account executive's. There are no shortcuts. Know the client. Know their product. Know their market. It will pay off.

Insist on a tight strategy.

Creative director Norman Berry wrote: "English strategies are very tight, very precise. Satisfy the strategy and the idea cannot be faulted even though it may appear outrageous. Many strategies are often too vague, too open to interpretation. 'The strategy for this product is taste,' they'll say. But that is not a strategy. Vague strategies inhibit. Precise strategies liberate."

You need a tight strategy.

On the other hand, a strategy can become too tight. When there's no play in the wheel, an overly specific strategy demands a very narrow range of executions and becomes, by proxy, an execution itself. Good account executives and account planners can fine-tune a strategy by moving it up and down a continuum between broad, meaningless statements and little pursed-lipped creative dictums masquerading as strategies.

Make sure what you have to say matters.

It must be relevant. It must matter to somebody, somewhere. It has to offer something customers want or solve a problem they have, whether it's a car that won't start or a drip that won't stop.

If you don't have something relevant to say, tell your client to put their wallets away.

Because no matter how well you execute it, an unimportant message has no receiver. The tree falls in the forest.

Find the central truth about your product.

Find the central truth about your whole product category. The central human truth. Hair coloring isn't about looking younger. It's about self-esteem. Cameras aren't about pictures. They're about stopping time and holding life as the sands run out.

There are ads to be written all around the edges of any product. But get to the ones written right from the essence of the thing.

Build a tension into your strategy.

Too often—no, in fact pretty much all the time—strategies seem to be little more than "themes" They create the illusion of a compelling idea but they're little more than that hand-lettered sign we all saw over our high school's gym door at prom: "A Night in Paris." Or "Fantasy Under the Sea." It's just a theme. Better, I think would be strategies that are built on top of, and powered by, cultural tensions. Example: Apple. For years, Apple has positioned itself as the "computer for the rest of us." The computer made for human beings, not for corporations. They've been riding this tension since their famous "1984" spot all the way up to their latest campaign, "Mac Guy versus PC Guy." Depending on the client being pitched, basing the strategy on a cultural tension isn't always possible. But when it is, great work is built into the strategy and fairly bursts out of it, like volcanoes built along tectonic plates.

Let your subconscious mind do it.

Where do ideas come from? I have no earthly idea. Around 1900, a writer named Charles Haanel said true creativity comes from "a benevolent stranger, working on our behalf." Novelist Isaac Bashevis Singer said, "There are powers who take care of you, who send you patience and stories." And film director Joe Pytka said, "Good ideas come from God." I think they're probably all correct. It's not so much our coming up with great ideas as it is creating a canvas where a painting can appear.

Stop the chatter in your head. Go into what author Joseph Heller called a "controlled daydream." Breathe from your stomach. If you're lucky, sometimes the ideas just begin to appear. What does the ad want to say? Not you, the ad. Shut up. Listen.

Try writing down words from the product's category.

You're selling outboard engines. Start a list on the side of the page: Fish. Water. Pelicans. Flotsam. Jetsam. Atlantic. Titanic. Ishmael.

What do these words make you think of? Pick up two of them and put them together like Tinkertoys. You have to start somewhere. Sure, it sounds stupid. The whole creative process is stupid.

It's like washing a pig. It's messy, it has no rules, no clear beginning, middle, or end; it's kind of a pain in the ass, and when you're done, you're not sure if the pig is clean or even why you were washing a pig in the first place.

Welcome to the creative department.

Be visual and go short on the copy.

The screensaver on the computers at London's Bartle Bogle Hegarty reads: "Words are a barrier to communication." Creative director John Hegarty says, "I just don't think people read ads."

I don't think most people read ads, either, at least not the body copy. There's a reason they say a picture is worth a thousand words.

Granted, if you interest a reader with a good visual or headline, yes, they may go on to read your copy. But the point is, you should try to solve the problem visually if you can.

Relying on one simple visual means it assumes added responsibilities and a bigger job description. You can't bury your main selling idea down in the copy. If the reader doesn't get what you're trying to say from the visual, he won't get it. The page is turned.

Don't take my word for it. Watch someone in the airport read a magazine. They whip through (usually backwards) at about two seconds per page. They glance at the clock on the wall. They turn a page. They think about the desperate, pimpled loneliness of their high school years. They look at a page. They see your ad.

If you can get them to take in your visual (or read your headline), your ad is a *resounding* success. Break out the Champale. Call your parents. You are a genius.

Get the visual clichés out of your system right away.

Certain visuals are just old. Somewhere out there is a Home for Tired Old Visuals. Sitting there in rocking chairs on the porch are visuals like Uncle Sam, a devil with a pitchfork, and a proud lion, just rocking back and forth waiting for someone to use them in an ad once again. And grousing. "When we were young, we were in all kinds of ads. People used to love us."

It's good to pay a short visit to the icons at the Home for Tired Old Visuals. Tell them you really liked their stuff when you first saw them in '84. And when you saw them in 1985. Loved you in '86. You still had it in '87, baby. They will nod off after a while. This is when you sneak away, never to return.

Move back and forth between wide-open, blue-sky thinking and critical analysis.

It's like this: Up there in my brain, there's this poet guy. Smokes a lot. Wears black. He's so creative. And "chicks dig 'im." He's got a million ideas. But 999,000 of them suck. He knows this because there's also a certified public accountant up there who tells him so.

"That won't work. You suck."

The CPA is a no-nonsense guy who clips coupons and knows how to fix the car when the poet runs it into the ditch on his way to "Beret World."

Between the two of them, though, I manage to come up with a few ideas that actually work.

The trick is to give each one his say. Let the poet go first. Be loose. Be wild. Then let the CPA come in, take measurements, and just bow out here by saying go back and forth between wild dorm-room creativity and Dad's basement analysis, always keeping your strategy statement in mind.

Make the claim in your ad something that is uncontestable. When you have a fact at your command, use it. When you can say, "This product lasts 20 years," what's to argue with? State fact, not manufactured nonsense about, oh, say, how "We Put the 'Qua' in Quality."

Come up with a lot of ideas. Cover the wall.

It's tempting to think that the best advertising people just peel off great campaigns ten minutes before they're due. But that is perception, not reality.

In fact, "Perception/Reality" (the famous *Rolling Stone* campaign from Fallon McElligott) is a perfect case in point. Those great ads that you may have seen in all the awards annuals are only the tip of the iceberg.

The rest of it, a four-foot-high pile of other layouts, sat in the writer, Bill Miller's, office for years. So massive was the pile of ideas, what he didn't use as ads actually served as a small table.

As a creative person, you will discover your brain has a built-in tendency to want to reach closure, even rush to it.

Evolution has left us with circuitry that doesn't like ambiguity or unsolved problems. Its pattern-recognition wiring evolved to keep us out of the jaws of lions, tigers, and bears—not for making lateral jumps to discover unexpected solutions.

But in order to get to a great idea, which is usually the 500th one to come along, you'll need to resist the temptation to give into the anxiety and sign off on the first passable idea that shows up.

Write hot. Edit cold.

Get it on paper, fast furious. Be hot. Let it pour out.

Don't edit anything when you're coming up with the ads.

Then later, be ruthless. Cut everything that is not A+ work. Put all the A- and B+ stuff off in another pile you'll revisit later. Everything that's B- or below, put on the shelf for emergencies.

"The wastepaper basket is the writer's best friend."—Isaac Bashevis Singer

Eschew obfuscation.

Get puns out of your system right away.

Puns, in addition to being the lowest thing on the joke food-chain, have no persuasive value. It's okay to think them. It's okay to write them down. Just make sure you toss them.

Certain headlines are currently checked out. You may use them when they are returned.

Lines like "Contrary to popular belief…" or "Something is wrong when…" These are dead. Elvis is dead. Deal with it.

Remember, anything that you even think you've seen, forget about. The stuff you've never seen? You'll know that when you see it, too. It raises the hair on the back of your neck.

Sweat the details.

Don't let even the smallest thing slide.

If it bothers you, work on it until it doesn't.

"A poem is never finished, only abandoned."—Paul Valery

Kill off the weak sister.

If your campaign has even one sort-of-okay ad in it, replace it with one as great as the others. Good is the enemy of great.

Remember that you aren't saving lives.

When you get stressed and the walls are closing in and you're going nuts trying to crack a problem and you find yourself getting depressed, try to remember that you're just doing an ad. That is all. It's just an ad. Bertrand Russell said, *"One of the symptoms of an approaching nervous breakdown is the belief that one's work is terribly important."*

Don't drink or do drugs.

You may think that drinking, smoking pot, or doing coke makes you more creative. I used to think so, too. In a business where we all purport to avoid clichés, a lot of people buy into this cliché-as-lifestyle. I can assure you it is illusion.

Keep your eye on the ball, not on the players.

Don't get into office politics. Not all offices have them. If yours does, remember your priority—doing ads. Keep your eye on the ad on your desk.

You are a member of a team.

Never get into the "I did the visual" or "I did the headline" thing. You work as a team, you lose as a team, you win as a team.

You are not genetically superior to account executives.

During my first years in the business I was trained to look down on AEs. At the time it seemed kind of cool to have a bad guy to make fun of. ("Oh, he couldn't sell a joint at Woodstock." "She couldn't sell a compass to Amelia Earhart.") But I was an idiot. It's wrong to think that way. They are on my side. Make sure they are on yours.

Don't let advertising mess up your life.

I must warn you against working to the exclusion of all else. We all seem to take this silly advertising stuff so seriously.

Some of us end up working way too hard and ignoring our spouses, our partners, our friends, and our lives. Remember, ultimately, it's just advertising. Compared to the important things in life, even a commercial that runs on the Super Bowl is still just an overblown coupon ad for Jell-O. Love, happiness, stability, sanity—those are the important things. Don't forget it.

Don't underestimate yourself.

Don't think, "I shouldn't bother sending my book to that agency. They're too good."

All people are subject to low self-esteem, and I think creative people are particularly prone to it. I can think of several people in our creative department who didn't think they were "good enough," but sent their book on a lark and we took them up on it.

Don't overestimate yourself.

For some reason, a lot of people in this business develop huge egos. Yet none of us is saving lives. We are glorified sign painters and nothing more.

Stay humble.

LUKE SULLIVAN HAS BEEN IN THE BUSINESS OVER THIRTY YEARS, WITH STINTS AT BOZELL & JACOBS, DELLA FEMINA, THE MARTIN AGENCY, AND FALLON IN HIS HOMETOWN OF MINNEAPOLIS. HE IS NOW AT GSDM IN AUSTIN, TEXAS. THIS ESSAY IS AN EXCERPT FROM HIS WONDERFUL BOOK, *HEY WHIPPLE, SQUEEZE THIS: A GUIDE TO CREATING GREAT ADS*, © 2008. REPRODUCED WITH PERMISSION OF JOHN WILEY & SONS, INC.

LOGIC TO MAGIC

BY ERIC WEBER

One of our favorite creative people

The creative process is hard. It's *hard* to think up great work…and once thought up, it's hard to sell to clients.

A question I am constantly being asked is, "How does a creative person think up great work? How does it actually happen in a creative person's head?"

In my mind, the Creative Process is the leaping from the Logic of a sound strategy to the Magic of an extraordinary execution that makes one internalize and believe the strategic proposition. The strategy is crucial; I believe in primitive, fundamental, non-esoteric strategies because I am certain that advertising *has* to be very fundamental.

I remember a speculative ad for Tonka toys done by a young man named Harold Kaplan.

I first saw this ad in Harold's original portfolio, and kept a Xerox of it over the years because I think it's a superb example of the leap from Logic to Magic.

Harold had been given the assignment of proving that Tonka toys last. That, in fact, is the theme line in the ad—"Tonka Toys Last." If, however, Tonka had run an ad that showed a picture of a Tonka truck with the headline "Tonka Toys Last," parents might think, *Maybe, possibly, or Yeah, I kind of know that.*

Harold started with Logic and created Magic. The picture, which is very crudely drawn, is of a little boy dropping a truck.

The headline says, "Tonka Toys Can't Fly, But They Sure Can Land." Same idea, same strategy, but delivered in a truly magical way. I suspect that if parents saw *that* ad in a magazine they would believe the idea and internalize it vastly more than if the ad simply said, "Tonka Toys Last."

That, to me, in a nutshell, is what advertising is all about; that's the mystery and the magic of it. It's what creative people have to try to do every moment of their working and perhaps waking lives. The goal is simple; the accomplishing of it hard.

One might legitimately ask, "Well, is it worth it? Why not just run solid advertising that's clear and on strategy and get on with it?" I'll tell you why.

Let's draw from the annals of advertising and look at a couple of examples where the leap from Logic to Magic has yielded the most extraordinary business success, generating billions upon billions of dollars for clients. First, I will relate a little anecdote that has really crystallized some of my strongest feelings about advertising.

A number of years ago, I created a new campaign for Molson beer. It said, "In Canada, winter comes a little earlier, the snows mount a little higher, the rivers run a little swifter. Some people say you can taste it in the beer." Perhaps you remember it.

I was very proud of that campaign, and so every couple of weeks I would go down to the candy/magazine/beer store in town and I'd ask the owner, Ed Lazzara, who was a bit of a marketing genius in his own right, how Molson was selling. "Well, Eric, for an import beer it sells pretty well, but you know what really sells in my store? Three products. In fact, if I had to do it all over again, I'd open little kiosks all over the Northeast and sell only three products."

According to Lazzara, those three products are Coca-Cola Classic at lunch, Budweiser beer on Friday evening and for the weekend, and Marlboro cigarettes right here in the shirt pocket. Every construction crew, every college kid with a summer job, every middle-aged insurance salesmen—Bud, Coke, and Marlboro.

I found this really fascinating because over the last three decades or so these three products have had extraordinary advertising.

Think about it: "Coke Is It," Mean Joe Green. "The Real Thing," Max Headroom. "I'd like to buy the world a Coke." For Budweiser, the two farmers cheering the Olympic torchbearer. "For all you do this Bud's for you." Spuds. "Give me a light." The immigrant carpenter being initiated into Americanhood with a Bud—extraordinary, uplifting, advertising.

And of course Marlboro Country, which took what was considered a girls' cigarette in the '50s and turned it into a boys' cigarette in a few short years. That one campaign, which ran for close to three decades, has generated so much money that Philip Morris, which was a small U.S. tobacco company, has been able to buy Miller beer, General Foods, and Kraft Foods, making it a true global marketing giant.

And what has funded it? Marlboro Country.

What interests me in particular about the advertising of these three great brands is the extraordinary added value it has brought to what are in reality some pretty mundane products. Think about it. Cola. A sugary, sweet liquid with bubbles in it. Beer. Mead, man's oldest and, next to water, most common drink. And tobacco…which, with all due respect to our client Philip Morris, doesn't exactly improve one's time in the 100-yard dash.

And yet America, and the world, views these three products with the most powerful and positive feelings. Why? I submit, primarily, because of the superior advertising they've had year in and year out.

Patriotism, masculinity, friendliness, popularity, attractiveness, wholesomeness—all these positive traits are associated with these great brands because of what has been projected in their advertising.

What consistency! What brilliance!

Whose inspiration was it to link a cola to youthful, active, tribal America? To link beer with working men's camaraderie? To link a filtered cigarette with the independence and ruggedness of the cowboy?

We've come to accept these connections as perfectly natural. But somewhere, a creative person made the leap from the Logic of a dry strategic document to magical, inspirational, motivating feelings and thoughts…and then, even more significantly, a client bought it, approved it, went with it.

Now think about other businesses. Maybe there is a way to make a connection between any product and the way people want to see themselves, the way they want to feel. I liked the Apple line, "The power to be your best." It's just a computer, and somehow they've got me excited about my whole life, because I have the power to be my best. (And today, I like to "Think Different." It's still magic.)

I want to relate one case in which I went from Logic to Magic, to give you a little clearer picture of how it actually happens in a creative person's head. A number of years ago Frank DeVito, president/creative director of Lintas, asked me to help on one of his accounts. *"Eric, I need your help. I have a crisis on Dr. Pepper."*

We were both associate creative directors at Y&R, handling a lot of business. Dr. Pepper was one of Frank's accounts, and I agreed to help him out.

We didn't have any time during the day, so we met for dinner every night for a week straight, three or four hours each night, and we made Dr. Pepper commercials. Dr. Pepper was the most glamorous account at Y&R at the time, and it still arguably is, so we felt we had to do some really terrific stuff.

This was the strategy: *You will enjoy the deliciously unique, increasingly popular taste of Dr. Pepper.* Frank and I came up with a lot of good stuff, but none of it felt MAGICAL. About the fifth or sixth night of working—we'd had a bottle of wine and were getting a little crazy—Frank said, "How about a couple of tough teenage girls walking along, wearing jackets that say *Peppers* on the back—like it's a gang?" Then he quickly said, "No, that's stupid."

I said, "I don't think it's stupid—what if everybody who drinks Dr. Pepper IS a Pepper? You know, like, *Be a Pepper.* Peppers are lively, peppery, spicy individualistic people."

"Be a Pepper." What an idea! We knew, after nearly a week of working, that we had pulled the Magic out of the Logic... that we had struck gold.

I hope I have given you some idea of how creative people actually get from Logic to Magic. Of course, after we *got* that far, we still had the great challenge of selling the campaign, which we obviously also lived to tell about.

I'd like to shift gears now and tell you about a lesson I recently learned when I let someone else take the leap from Logic to Magic.

After my wife and I had our fourth kid, the house suddenly began to feel small. My daughters both came down to the kitchen one morning sobbing, "We hate each other, and we can't stand being in the same room." So we decided we would end the sibling wars by adding on a bedroom.

Now, I'm a practical Head of Household, and I didn't want to spend a lot of money. I also know how architects can lose control, especially in collusion with wives who have *Architectural Digest*-scale dreams.

So I said, "Roland"—I knew the architect—"I want it over here; I want it to be a box. I want it to be very basic. I don't want any fancy roofs, gargoyles, anything. A box."

Fortunately, I got extremely busy at work and the architect and my wife forged ahead with their own plans. I was horrified when I saw them. I thought their ideas were impractical and totally excessive.

I didn't know why I needed some stupid connection between the box and the house... and I knew it would cost me more.

Fortunately, I was very busy at work. In a moment of total distraction, I said, "All right, go ahead and do it."

Am I happy I did! I know now that if I'd gotten what I'd asked for, I'd have gotten something that I didn't particularly want. I got something I didn't ask for, which made me a little uncomfortable at first, but I have really come to love it—it's added an enormous amount of aesthetic and, I suspect, financial value to my house.

I didn't control the Magic. I let it happen.

ERIC WEBER, FOUNDER AND HEAD OF THE TENAFLY FILM COMPANY, BEGAN HIS CAREER AS A COPYWRITER AND HAS CREATED DOZENS OF AMERICA'S BEST-KNOWN AD CAMPAIGNS, INCLUDING "BE A PEPPER" FOR DR PEPPER AND "IT'S AN UP THING" FOR 7-UP. HE WAS EXECUTIVE CREATIVE DIRECTOR AT YOUNG & RUBICAM IN NEW YORK AND FOOTE, CONE & BELDING IN CHICAGO, AND HAS WON NUMEROUS INDUSTRY AWARDS, INCLUDING A GOLD AND SILVER LION AT CANNES. IN ADDITION TO HIS ADVERTISING WRITING, ERIC HAS WRITTEN AND DIRECTED THREE FILMS, INCLUDING *SUITS*, STARRING ROBERT KLEIN, WHICH DEPICTS THE WAR BETWEEN THE SUITS AND THE CREATIVES IN AN ADVERTISING AGENCY.

AFTERWORD

Keynote address to the Miami Ad School graduating class, by Maxine Paetro

First, I want to congratulate you for working so hard and for graduating tonight. As I look out at all of you, I know you're wondering, maybe worrying, about your future.

I've interviewed many thousands of graduates as they've stood on the brink of who-knows-what. And I want to be among the first to tell you that things are going to be very different when you leave school and get your first job in advertising.

Things won't necessarily be better or worse, but life will be more real, because your school experience is quite different from what life will be like when you have a job.

Right now, what's going on for you in school is about you; it's about your ads, your book, and your job potential. When you step outside these doors and join an advertising agency, it is not going to be about you anymore. There will be many more people involved in "your" ad, a cast of dozens, because the end result will be analyzed, judged, and paid for by the client, who may be spending many millions for advertising that must pay off in sales of product or services.

I want to tell you about a time when I was the administrative head of the creative department and as such the creative recruiter at Saatchi & Saatchi—a very large agency that almost no one wanted to work for. And the reason that no one wanted to work at Saatchi & Saatchi and agencies like Saatchi & Saatchi—that is to say big agencies with *big account clients*—was that they thought they weren't going to get to do very good work at those places.

They thought they'd be doing cereal ads and detergent commercials and that they couldn't win awards with those kinds of ads. And if they were unable to do award-winning advertising, their careers would go down the drain.

And because of this kind of thinking, under most circumstances, an agency like ours probably couldn't have attracted as many good people as it did. But we had a secret weapon.

Within Saatchi & Saatchi was a small division, a group of very talented people who were winning awards for a hamburger chain and a long-life light bulb.

The agency was Cliff Freeman & Partners.

In fact *all* the people who worked at Saatchi & Saatchi had talent, but Cliff Freeman's group had the kind of talent that was rewarded with statues, and that was the kind of talent that attracted kids from schools like this one, and we wanted you guys.

So we set up a recruitment and training program, and it was my mission at the time to bring as many good young people as we possibly could and expose them to advertising and pick their brains and have them infuse the agency with their vision of what they thought the world was going to be like and how they saw products and how they connected with people their own age.

Our ultimate goal, of course, was to hold on to some number of these kids, who would become true assets to the agency and a real part of the company going into the future.

I'm going to use the word "kids" a lot. I can't help it; it's how we think of you guys. I hope you understand that it is a term that we use with a great deal of affection.

Anyway, over the course of five years, we hired fifty kids.

That was a while ago, but I still remember those kids, every single one of them. And this will interest you because it goes to the heart of what you're all wondering now. What will happen to me? What will happen if I take the wrong job? Where will I be two or ten or fifteen years from now?

Here's what happened to those fifty kids who were very much like you are today.

First, it's interesting but not surprising that the largest number of the kids that came out of that program have been very successful by any standards—that is to say, many are secure, doing work that is often satisfying, and they're making over $250,000 a year.

It's not surprising because these were talented kids, and it would almost have been harder for them to fail than succeed. And succeed they did.

Fifteen years after graduating from our training program, five of those former kids were still at Saatchi & Saatchi, and that meant mutual satisfaction between themselves and the agency over the long haul.

One of these former trainees, a particularly shy young man, was an executive vice president, heading a division that has to do with advertising to children, and this is a special interest of his.

Another one of those kids was a brain when it comes to new technology. He was chosen to head a division that has to do with the Web and interactive TV.

The other three are also respected ad people with solid careers.

Four of the kids from the first group were scooped up immediately by Cliff Freeman & Partners, and they stayed for a number of years and almost immediately started getting awards, the good kind: lions that come in a box lined with velvet.

It was pretty damned thrilling, let me tell you, to go to the Cannes Film Festival in New York and see young people that I had interviewed when they were sitting in groups like this, going up to collect their awards.

One of our kids wanted to go back to Hungary, where he was born, and Saatchi sent him. He lived his dream to be a creative director of an entire office, and then he came back to the United States, and he is doing well.

While some of our kids stayed at Saatchi for their entire careers, others found similar large agency homes and have not moved from them. One team stayed at Y&R for twelve years, another spent thirteen years at DMB&B. Another is a lifer at Leo Burnett.

One of those original kids became a creative director of a soft drink account at another gigantic agency, and quit because he had other interests. He went off to California and started a business of his own, then came back to New York to work for Spike Lee. He's made a film I've seen on the Sundance channel, and at this writing he's teaching advertising at a respected university.

Several of the others got jobs in smaller agencies throughout the country, and others, notably a writer/writer team who got married a few years back, made careers of being professional freelancers.

Three—count 'em, three—of our kids became hugely successful commercial TV directors on a short list of best directors in New York. Two of them were from our first group of ten.

The third came to the agency a year later. I remember him well because he was so talented it was scary and he was also very attractive. But instead of getting lost in the social opportunities in New York City—he stayed home most nights to work on improving his book— even though he already had a great job.

This young art director left Cliff Freeman after a few years, went to work at another big agency, won some awards, became a little disillusioned with the reality of advertising, and then he got over it. As I said, he became a director, and last I heard he was doing very, very well.

Over the twenty years following their entry into advertising, nearly every one of Saatchi's former trainees distinguished himself or herself with statues, titles, and those big pay checks I've told you about.

But some of them took time off, stepped out, gathered their thoughts and figured out what they were going to do next. Some resurfaced a year or two later and went back into advertising. Some opted out for good because they knew advertising wasn't for them.

One very precocious young woman dropped out in the middle of the training program. I was trying to expand our program to our offices overseas, and after this young woman started her rotation in our London office, she decided she wanted to see France! So she quit. I didn't forgive her easily for doing this, because that was a pilot international program and I wanted all my kids to get circulated through European offices.

Anyway, she quit, and then maybe a year later she was rehired by the agency at three times her former salary and moved up the ladder as well. Years later, she quit again, went to a few other agencies, and now is selling real estate in East Hampton. She got a call just last week; an agency wanting to hire her for a lucrative freelance assignment. She said, "No, thanks, I'm not interested."

One of our kids co-wrote a screenplay two years after graduating from our training program. He and his teammate sold it for $400,000, which is about a million in today's dollars. As far as I know, this former advertising trainee is still out in Hollywood and he is still writing screenplays.

One of our kids just got his own syndicated cartoon column. Another has a big career as a fine artist. Another of our former trainees wrote to me recently to tell me that after fifteen years as a creative director, he ditched it all and bought himself a tiny house on a tiny island in the South Pacific.

He's eating fruit that tastes like candy, sleeping in a hammock, and thinking things over.

Not all of the kid stories have happy endings.

A couple of our wunderkind got busted out of our business because they were arrogant and had bad business manners, and actually I kind of knew they had bad business manners and that they where arrogant when I participated in the decision to hire them.

But I didn't really care because I didn't think it was going to be a problem. I thought that I could keep my hand on the reins and help them and teach them. In a way I guess that was my arrogance that I thought I could do that.

I remember one of them in particular. He was a rule-breaker, and we kind of liked rule-breakers in this business then, and maybe now, too. Back then, in order to get in the training program he had to submit a test as well as his portfolio. There was a deadline, and this kid decided that the date of the deadline was midnight, not the end of business day.

He convinced the security guard to let him into my office at midnight, not a good thing. The security guard involved got in trouble, and even my secretary asked me not to consider this kid whatsoever, he was such a bad kid.

I took a chance and guess what: He was in trouble every single day. He was contentious, difficult, and told everybody else that his work was brilliant and that theirs was crap. But he was great in his way. It's funny because there was an endearing side to him, and he was one of those who quit and came back to the agency more than once. Too late to make a long story short, but to tell you the ending, this kid married an exceptional art director, a better art director than he was. And he achieved some maturity in the long run.

The other youngster who led with his arrogance was also endearing, a little broken, and demonstrably talented.

Two years after hiring him, he told me he was a convicted felon. That was after he convinced an account executive to let him direct a television commercial when he actually had no idea what he was doing. Luckily it was a commercial for a local retail account, but still, tens of thousands of dollars later, the agency had unusable film and had to eat the cost.

The kid got pulled down from his high horse, and he truly never recovered his reputation at our agency. He dropped out of sight, and last I heard he was sleeping under the Santa Monica Pier. I guess you could say he pretty much washed out of the business.

Some of our kids who dropped out of advertising went off our radar. One of our kids became a heroin addict. Others got married, moved away, became tennis pros, or I just don't know what happened to them, but chances are, they are having very good lives.

In sum, all fifty of those kids were very bright and very talented.

Every one of those kids started their advertising career with a great book and a squeaking clean endorsement and went to work in an agency most didn't want to admit to their friends.

Why some didn't work out and why some did, leads me to conclude something.

The first job you get is not as important as you think it is.

I know from meeting some 30,000 beginners, talking to them as I look at their books, that this is what you're thinking: "If I don't get hired by Fallon (or whatever the agency of your dreams is), life is over." It's not true.

Fifty kids like you. Half of them have done extraordinary well in advertising, another 25% have been successful in a related field. The other 25% have left advertising forever, where they either crashed or found happiness in some other kind of work.

So, what I think is more important than your first job is who you are as a person.

You've heard the expression "It's only advertising," and it's not an expression you really want to hear when you are working a hundred hours a week on your book and projecting fantasies of your life in advertising.

But advertising is a business, and your life is your life.

Your real job from this moment on is to make your life as long and as rich as you can make it.

So this is my advice: When you get that first job, whatever it is, work hard at it. Respect the agency that hires you and the people who give you your first chance. There are talented people everywhere, so take the time to learn from them and to give them more than they hoped or expected from you.

Do things for others, and I don't really mean in the agency itself. Do something that has to do with giving, because there are going to be times when you're sitting at your desk trying to define yourself by doing an ad for a product that seems to have a negative value in the world, or you'll be working with someone you dislike, and it would really be a good idea if you had something in your mind that reminded you that you are not only a copywriter, art director, designer.

That you are also a person who took a kid to the park or delivered meals on wheels or made sure to call home every Sunday.

It's also a good idea to develop other interests, feed your mind, and be a good friend.

And lastly, most of you will get that job in advertising that fueled your dreams and brought you to this school—or you will find a path that suits you even better.

Keep the faith. Henry David Thoreau said it best: "If one advances confidently in the direction of his dreams, and endeavors to live the life which he has imagined, he will meet with a success unexpected in common hours."

Thank you for listening.

I wish you all the best of everything.

READING & RESOURCES

Compiled with the help of George Felton

MAGAZINES

All these magazines have extensive Web sites, often with access to back issues, podcasts, blogs, newsletters, and other resources.

Advertising Age

www.adage.com

Adweek

www.adweek.com

Both of these weekly magazines keep you abreast of advertising—agencies, accounts, clients, and trends.

Brandweek

www.brandweek.com

CMYK

www.cmykmag.com

A magazine dedicated to student work, with lots of advice for young creatives. Invaluable if you're just getting started.

Communication Arts

www.commarts.com/CA

CA is a bible to many creatives, widely used and often cited.

Creativity Online

http://creativity-online.com/

In 2009 Creativity magazine became a Web-only resource, Creativity Online. It's an excellent source for the latest ad campaigns in all media, as well as interviews, reviews, and news.

Fast Company

www.fastcompany.com

A business magazine with lots of marketing and advertising relevance.

Graphis

www.graphis.com

Magazine of visual communications, international in scope.

HOW

www.howdesign.com

A graphic arts magazine with a "how-to" bent.

I.D.

www.id-mag.com

Deals with all kinds of design—product, package, graphic, etc.

Inc.

www.inc.com

Another business magazine read by many advertising and marketing people.

Lurzer's Archive
(Everyone just calls it "Archive.")

www.luerzersarchive.us

Published bimonthly. Excellent collection of cutting-edge international work.

One. a Magazine

www.oneclub.org

Published by the One Club. Handsome, oversized quarterly with high-quality editorial content.

Print

www.printmag.com

A venerable magazine whose title is a misnomer: it's about design in all its forms. Includes the Regional Design Annual, which presents the best work from each region of the U.S.

WIRED

www.wired.com

Published monthly. Important writing on the future of advertising and technology.

BOOKS ON PORTFOLIOS

Mine may have been the first, but it's no longer the only one. Some of these emphasize portfolios for art directors or designers.

Baron, Cynthia L.
Designing a Digital Portfolio, Second Edition.
Berkeley: New Riders-Peachpit, 2009.

Eisenman, Sara.
Building Design Portfolios: Innovative Concepts for Presenting Your Work.
Gloucester, MA: Rockport, 2006.

Holloway, Dave.
How to Get the Advertising Job You Want.
Seattle: Holloway, 2009.

Linton, Harold.
Portfolio Design, Third Edition.
New York: W. W. Norton, 2004.

Vonk, Nancy, and Janet Kestin.
Pick Me: Breaking into Advertising and Staying There.
New York: Adweek-Wiley, 2005.

AWARD BOOKS

ADDY Award Books

Most ad clubs publish books that salute the winners of their local and regional ADDY competitions. Check with your local ad club to track one down. (The Minneapolis book has been particularly good. Miami's ADDYs were where Crispin first made its name.)

Art Directors Annual

www.adcglobal.org

Highly regarded annual of advertising and design from the Art Directors Club in New York.

Communication Arts Annuals

www.commarts.com

The Communication Arts Advertising Annual is a favorite; other annuals, now folded into the bimonthly issues, are *Design, Photography, Interactive*, and *Illustration*.

D&AD Annual

www.dandad.org

British.

One Show, One Show Design,
and One Show Interactive annuals
www.oneclub.org

Published by the One Club. Every year *The One Show* sponsors a college competition, whose winners are published in the annual. If you're still in school, enter it.

BASIC BOOKSHELF

These books are generally regarded as useful and are generally available—though you may have to look on a used book site. There are new books coming out all the time—go to a superstore or check the Web stores.

Aitchison, Jim.
Cutting Edge Advertising II: How to Create the World's Best Print for Brands in the 21st Century, Second Edition.
Singapore: Prentice-Hall, 2003.

Applegate, Edd, ed.
The Ad Men and Women: A Biographical Dictionary of Advertising.
Westport, CT: Greenwood, 1994.

(A reference book, really, with well-researched biographies of fifty-four important advertising people of the 19th and 20th centuries.)

The Art Direction Book.
Mies, Switzerland: Designers and Art Directors Association of the United Kingdom and Rotovision SA, 1997.

(Companion volume to *The Copy Book*.)

Barry, Pete.
The Advertising Concept Book: Think Now, Design Later.
New York: Thames & Hudson, 2008.

Bendinger, Bruce.
The Copy Workshop Workbook, Fourth Edition.
Chicago: Copy Workshop, 2009.

Berger, Warren.
Advertising Today.
New York: Phaidon, 2001.

The Copy Book: How 32 of the World's Best Advertising Writers Write Their Advertising.
Mies, Switzerland: Designers and Art Directors Association of the United Kingdom and Rotovision SA, 1995.

Crispin Porter + Bogusky and Warren Berger.
Hoopla.
Brooklyn, NY: powerHouse, 2006.

(The amazing adventures of CP+B.)

Dru, Jean-Marie.
Disruption: Overturning Conventions and Shaking Up the Marketplace.
New York: Adweek-Wiley, 1996.

Fallon, Pat, and Fred Senn.
Juicing the Orange.
Boston: Harvard Business School Press, 2006.
(How they think and work at Fallon.)

Fallon, Pat, and Bob Barrie.
The Work: 25 Years of Fallon.
Minneapolis: Fallon Worldwide, 2006.

Felton, George.
Advertising Concept and Copy, Second Edition.
New York: W. W. Norton, 2006.

Fox, Stephen.
The Mirror Makers.
Champaign: University of Illinois Press, 1997.
(Great book on the early days of advertising.)

Goldberg, Natalie.
Writing Down the Bones, Expanded Edition.
Boston: Shambhala, 2005.
(Widely admired approach to writing.)

Gossage, Howard, et al.
The Book of Gossage.
Chicago: Copy Workshop, 2006.
(Unique insights from one of advertising's true originals.)

Hale, Constance.
Sin and Syntax: How to Craft Wickedly Effective Prose.
New York: Broadway, 2001.

Higgins, Denis.
The Art of Writing Advertising.
New York: McGraw-Hill, 2003.
(Interviews with William Bernbach, George Gribbin, Rosser Reeves, David Ogilvy, and Leo Burnett.)

Himpe, Tom.
Advertising Is Dead: Long Live Advertising!
New York: Thames & Hudson, 2006.
(Excellent examples and analysis of the many forms of non-traditional advertising.)

——. *Advertising Next: 150 Winning Campaigns for the New Communications Age.*
San Francisco: Chronicle, 2008.

Kessler, Stephen.
Chiat/Day: The First 20 Years.
New York: Rizzoli, 1990.
(A great look at a great agency.)

Kirshenbaum, Richard, and Jonathan Bond.
Under the Radar: Talking to Today's Cynical Consumer.
New York: Adweek-Wiley, 1998.

Landa, Robin.
Advertising by Design: Creating Visual Communications with Graphic Impact.
Hoboken, NJ: Wiley, 2004.

Levenson, Bob.
Bill Bernbach's Book.
New York: Villard, 1987.

Martin, David.
Romancing the Brand: The Power of Advertising and How to Use It.
New York: AMACOM, 1989.
(Martin is the founder of The Martin Agency.)

Minsky, Laurence.
How to Succeed in Advertising When All You Have Is Talent, Second Edition.
Chicago: Copy Workshop, 2007.
(Ad greats show and talk about the work that first got them work.)

Pricken, Mario.
Creative Advertising: Ideas and Techniques from the World's Best Campaigns, Second Edition.
New York: Thames & Hudson, 2008.
(Lots of terrific ads and the techniques used to create them.)

Redish, Janice.
Letting Go of the Words: Writing Web Content That Works.
Boston: Morgan Kaufmann, 2007.

Roman, Kenneth, and Jane Maas.
The New How to Advertise.
New York: St. Martin's, 1992.

Rothenberg, Randall.
Where the Suckers Moon: An Advertising Story.
New York: Knopf, 1994.
(The eye-opening story of Wieden + Kennedy's Subaru pitch and what happened after that.)

Stabiner, Karen.
Inventing Desire.
New York: Simon & Schuster, 1993.
(A year spent inside Chiat/Day.)

Steel, Jon.
Truth, Lies & Advertising: The Art of Account Planning.
New York: Adweek-Wiley, 1998.

Strunk, William, Jr., and E. B. White.
The Elements of Style, Fourth Edition.
New York: Longman, 2000.
(If you think you're a writer, you should have this. If you don't have it, get it.)

Sullivan, Luke.
Hey Whipple, Squeeze This!, Third Edition.
New York: Adweek-Wiley, 2008.
(Cited by nearly every advertiser around. Smart, funny, extremely useful.)

Twitchell, James B.
20 Ads That Shook the World.
New York: Three Rivers, 2000.

Usborne, Nick.
Net Words: Creating High-Impact Online Copy.
New York: McGraw-Hill, 2002.

Zinsser, William.
On Writing Well, 30th Anniversary Edition.
New York: HarperCollins, 2006.
(A classic on the craft of writing.)

GOLDEN OLDIES

Good books, but they usually give you a look at how the business used to be. You may have to search for some of them.

Bedell, Clyde.
How to Write Advertising That Sells.
New York: McGraw-Hill, 1940.
(An old-time classic.)

Buxton, Edward.
Creative People at Work.
New York: Executive Communications, 1975.

Caples, John.
How to Make Your Advertising Make Money.
Englewood Cliffs, NJ: Prentice-Hall, 1983.

———. *Tested Advertising Methods.*
Paramus, NJ: Prentice-Hall, 1997.

Cummings, Bart.
The Benevolent Dictators.
Lincolnwood, IL: NTC Business Books, 1987.
(Interviews with ad greats.)

Della Femina, Jerry.
From Those Wonderful Folks Who Brought You Pearl Harbor.
New York: Simon & Schuster, 1970.
(A lot of fun!)

Dobrow, Larry.
When Advertising Tried Harder: The Sixties, The Golden Age of American Advertising.
New York: Friendly, 1984.

Fulton, Sue, and Edward Buxton.
Advertising Freelancers, New Expanded Edition.
New York: Executive Communications, 1989.

Hopkins, Claude.
My Life in Advertising & Scientific Advertising.
Lincolnwood, IL: NTC Business Books, 1993.

Ogilvy, David.
Confessions of an Advertising Man.
London: Southbank, 2004.

———. *Ogilvy on Advertising.*
New York: Vintage, 1985.
(The one, the only, David Ogilvy. Read both books, if only to see what you disagree with.)

Reeves, Rosser.
Reality in Advertising.
New York: Knopf, 1961.
(The man who gave us the Unique Selling Proposition.)

Seiden, Hank.
Advertising Pure and Simple.
New York: AMACOM, 1990.

Watkins, Julius.
The 100 Greatest Advertisements, Revised and Enlarged Edition.
New York: Dover, 1959.
(Great ads from the early days.)

Young, James Webb.
A Technique for Producing Ideas.
Lincolnwood, IL: NTC Business Books, 1975.
(This little book is often cited by advertisers as among the best advice for thinking creatively.)

BUSINESS BOOKS

Here are some good books about marketing and advertising. Be sure to read at least one Trout and Ries book. Remember, advertising is a business.

Beckwith, Harry.
Selling the Invisible: A Field Guide to Modern Marketing.
New York: Warner, 1997.
(Readable marketing wisdom.)

Bogusky, Alex, and John Winsor.
Baked In: Creating Products and Businesses That Market Themselves.
Evanston, IL: Agate B2, 2009.

Drucker, Peter.
Managing for the Future.
New York: Dutton, 1992.
(Read something, anything, by Dr. Peter Drucker, one of the greatest business writers of all time.)

Gladwell, Malcolm.
The Tipping Point: How Little Things Can Make a Big Difference.
Boston: Little, Brown, 2002.
(All of Gladwell's books have marketing and advertising relevance. See his Web site, too: www.gladwell.com.)

Heath, Chip, and Dan Heath.
Made to Stick: Why Some Ideas Survive and Others Die.
New York: Random House, 2007.

Levitt, Theodore.
The Marketing Imagination. New, Expanded Edition.
New York: Free Press, 1986.

Ohmae, Kenichi.
The Mind of the Strategist.
New York: McGraw-Hill, 1991.

Ries, Al, and Jack Trout.
Bottom-Up Marketing.
New York: McGraw-Hill, 1989.

———. *Marketing Warfare.*
New York: McGraw Hill, 1986.

———. *Positioning: The Battle for Your Mind.*
New York: McGraw Hill, 1986.
(They invented the term. Must reading.)

———. *The 22 Immutable Laws of Marketing.*
New York: HarperBusiness, 1993.

BLOGS AND WEB SITES

These come and go more quickly than books and magazines. Here are some good current ones.

www.adfreak.com
Posts from Adweek writers.

www.adforum.com
Ads, ads, and more ads. Worldwide.

http://adland.tv
One of the first ad blogs, if not the first. Thousands of ads, many discussion boards, lots to explore.

www.adpulp.com
The advertising business, from the inside. Extensive links.

http://adsoftheworld.com
The URL says it all.

www.adverblog.com
Interactive advertising and marketing.

www.bannerblog.com.au
Showcases online advertising worldwide.

http://blog,wk.com
Wieden + Kennedy's blog (Portland office).

http://debmorrison.typepad.com

Deborah Morrison teaches advertising
at the University of Oregon. Lots on creativity
and ideas.

http://edwardboches.com

Edward Boches is chief creative officer at Mullen.

http://ihaveanidea.org

An abundance of advertising information, resources,
and, of course, ideas.

www.mediabistro.com

Resource center for all things media.

INDEX